ANTIQUE
COLOURED
GLASS

Antique Coloured
GLASS

Keith Middlemas

Ferndale Editions
London

This edition published 1979 by Ferndale Editions, London,
under licence from the proprietor

Copyright © 1971 by Barrie & Jenkins Ltd
All Rights Reserved

Photographs by Michael Plomer
© Barrie & Jenkins Ltd 1971

Printed in Italy by Nuova Grafica Moderna, Verona
Bound by Webb Son & Co. Ltd, London

Contents

Acknowledgements

I am greatly indebted to the following private collectors, institutions and antique dealers who have very kindly allowed me to take photographs of specimen glasses in their possession:

Corning Museum of Glass, New York

Mr. Richard Dennis

Mr. John Jesse

Mr. Howard Phillips

Mr. Leslie Scott

Messrs. Sotheby & Company

and to several of them for their good and helpful advice.

Introduction

The dramatic discovery, about the year 50 B.C., of the technique of blowing glass changed the whole art of glass making. Until then the skill of fusing silica with soda to make the clear metal, glass, was essentially akin to that of the lapidary, the carver of precious and semi-precious stones, which glass itself was at first intended to simulate. Even in Egypt, the centre of earliest glass making, where about 1400 B.C. workers began to pour the mixture over a core or cone of clay to form a vessel, often of considerable size, glass making remained a contrived and derivative technique. But when it became possible to dip a hollow rod, instead of a solid iron or pontil, into the furnace, gather a batch of ingredients on the end, and then blow out a flowing bubble and twist and manipulate it into any shape desired, glass making became an art and reached a stage comparable to that of the discovery of the wheel in the history of transport —so that in the two thousand years since, developments have been chiefly in the materials, the form and the colour of glass.

A brief account of the earliest origin of glass making was given in a previous volume, running from the first use of glass as a glaze in beads and tiles in pre-dynastic Egypt, to the Alexandrian period in the two centuries before the Roman conquest. Since this volume is concerned primarily with European glass of the period which may still be called collectable, as opposed to periods of which most of the surviving specimens are in museums, the Roman and Islamic epochs will be dealt with only briefly. But it should be emphasised that from the earliest uses of glass, colour was essential both as an ingredient of the material itself and as a form of decoration on the surface. Very little clear glass has survived from the remoter periods and the great majority of Roman pieces which are not deliberately coloured by the addition of mineral substances, is of the familiar pale green which is also the colour of almost all mediaeval European glass and of glass made in the vernacular tradition down to the 19th century.

Glass was made of sand, which was available in profusion in Europe, whether from the seashore or inland, and an alkali which had a more regional distribution. In Egypt it occurred as natron, available from the thousands of inland lakes along the North African coast, or else in the form of ash from the wood and leaves of marine plants. In mediaeval Europe, the latter was widely used: in Spain it was known as *barilla* and exported largely to Venice and Genoa; in the Rhine Valley and in northeast France it was made by burning bracken or beech wood, a manufacture which gave its name to the glass itself—*Waldglas* or *verre de fougère*. Thus, although the Roman empire helped to spread glass manufacture over most of Europe, it became an industry only where economic factors encouraged it, as had been true of Egypt, protected from war and disturbance and gifted with the necessary raw materials and high standard of living to maintain a skilled and luxurious art.

Until the addition of lime or chalk to the mixture in 17th century Germany, which made Bohemian and Silesian crystal possible, and of lead oxide in England in the 1670s, the body of glass was to be determined by these two basic ingredients. Soda glass remained light, bubbly and delicate, capable of marvellous forms in the hands of the expert glass blower, but subject to crizzelling (glass sickness) except in the most skilful hands. Whether it is sufficient explanation of the use of colour to say that the clear material was intrinsically unsatisfying before the 16th century in Venice, is a question which cannot be answered; but it was not until then, when the infinitely delicate shapes of glasses were determined by the lightness of the material, that a concerted attempt was made to decolourise the pale green which was caused by traces of iron in the silica. At this stage it was found that manganese oxide could be added to neutralise the effects of the iron.

Colour had been added deliberately for at least two thousand years before. Egyptian glass makers were familiar with many shades of blue and certain reds and yellows. Roman and Grecian fragments have been analysed, showing that early craftsmen were familiar with the use of several minerals and metallic oxides. Copper was used to make turquoise blue, the most favourite colour of antiquity, green, and also in Egypt, red; cobalt produced dark and light blue, and, mixed with a little iron, azure blue; iron and antimony could be mixed to include browns and yellows; manganese for amethyst and purple. The ancient world did not exhaust the combinations: in 17th-century Europe tin oxide or arsenic were added to produce opaque white glass, the *Milchglas* of Germany and Spain, as well as Bristol, and gold to make ruby red or pink; and in the 19th century came a whole range of surface stains made from copper salts and silver compounds; also black glass made with iron, and greenish yellow with uranium.

The method of manufacture, the fusing of the ingredients in a crucible or fire-clay pot, heated by wood, determined to some extent the regions in which early glass could be made before the extensive use of coal. Vast quantities of wood were necessary and even under the Roman empire, when transport and communications were far more efficient than in mediaeval Europe, glass making was an itinerant occupation, involving frequent moves in the forests in Gaul and in Germany. When European trade virtually broke down in the five hundred years after the collapse of Rome, this became another factor in the eventual development of distinct regional forms and traditions of glass making. But the chief factor in all the history of glass was the demand of the customer—for glass making before the era of mass production was a luxury profession. No greater contrast could be imagined between the magnificent stained glass windows produced for cathedrals such as Chartres and Bourges at the end of the 12th century and the primitive domestic glass ware of the same period. The church was a patron on the grand scale; six hundred years later the demands of the rich middle class of Germany were, equally, to create the age of Biedermeier in which, as in England in the mid-19th century, glass became for the first time a familiar household article in the houses of the people, rather than the mansions of the rich.

Roman Glass

Glass blowing was most probably invented at Sidon in Syria, where glass making had been established under Egyptian aegis since at least 1400 B.C. Syria became a province of Rome and Rome conquered Alexandria, the other principal centre, in 27 B.C. After the formation of the Empire under Augustus and his successors, glass manufacture spread into Italy itself, Gaul and Spain, until it covered the whole Empire by about A.D. 200. At first Alexandria, Italy and other Mediterranean centres such as Syracuse held the market for the luxury trade, while Syria, Gaul and the Rhineland produced glass for domestic and commercial needs. However, the northern glass houses challenged the Alexandrian supremacy and in the 3rd and 4th century sometimes surpassed it. The nature of Roman civilisation, the world image of its citizenship and the international character of its culture, gave a mobility to trade and manufacture which had never been previously known. A skilled workman could travel from Syria to the Rhineland and occupy himself in precisely the same occupation; even Britain was scarcely less civilised than southern France, as the vast scale of Fishbourne Palace, recently excavated at Chichester in Sussex, shows. The origin of Roman glassware is often difficult to determine, so general was the style.

Some clear glass was produced in Syria in the 2nd century A.D., using a decolourising agent, but the characteristic of all Roman glass is its colour. Domestic wares were usually green—in Syria a pale greenish blue, in Alexandria a darker green, in the Rhineland and Gaul a clear bright green. The finer products were coloured deliberately and here Roman glass reached a level of technical mastery not re-created until the 18th century in Europe: not only was a great variety of coloured vessels made, copying and improving on the earlier work of Egypt, but a number of wholly new developments took place. Most famous perhaps is the mosaic work, chiefly in bowls, called murrhine; but there were threads or ropes of white or coloured glass worked into the rims or the vessels themselves, foreshadowing the *latticino* work of Venice; lines of coloured glass trailed or raised with pincers as ropes on the body of the vessel; and, most intricate of all, the cameo carving, of which the most splendid example is the Portland Vase in the British Museum, in which a layer of opaque glass was laid over a deep blue coloured body and cut away in the classical figures which Wedgwood and then the 19th century English cameo cutters tried so hard to emulate.

Less elaborate decoration characterised the products of the factories north of Alexandria. The general class of Roman wares, large vessels for storage, bottles, two-handled vases and *amphorae*, drinking glasses and plates, dishes, lamps, mirrors and window glass, were scarcely less numerous than today. Nearly all were coloured, even the most commercial works often bearing decoration in the form of applied masks or ribbing, or splashes of abstract designs in opaque white glass. A monumental elegance distinguishes the best of them, such as the rectangular vase with a bold square handle illustrated in the previous volume. The cylindrical and angular pieces were mould blown; freely blown glass took smaller forms, such as phials, scent bottles, bowls, beakers and cups, and the long stemmed so-called 'tear bottles'.

By the second half of the Empire, the shapes of blown glass grew more elaborate and the makers launched out into the use of different colours for handles or rims. Later still, the shapes became elongated, freer and more fluid, with convoluted handles in the Syrian manner. The glass blower was breaking away from the strict canons of the imperial age, discovering a freedom in the blowing of his material and in the decoration. This has since been seen as a weakness. Indeed, the workmanship was often less precise and the material deteriorated in clarity and colour, but the change may be due more to the impact of Eastern religions on Europe after the age of the Antonine emperors, and the gradual inflow of barbarian habits into Gaul. Yet perhaps the finest of all Roman glass came at this time from the Rhineland, especially from Cologne which was the centre of the fashion for decorating with drops of coloured glass, like jewels; this was one of the few traditions to survive into mediaeval Europe. From here too, as well as Alexandria, came the most intricate and rare vases called *diatreta*: in which a solid mass of glass was cut away in great depth to leave a vessel with an outer network of interlaced circles, standing out from it like an infinitely complex halo.

In contrast to the sophistication of form and colour, painting on Roman glass often appears crude, but this is probably only the reaction of a differently attuned modern taste. Certainly, in technical advance, the Romans allowed nothing to 18th century Europe. Most of their painting was done in unfired oils and has consequently vanished, but a number of 3rd and 4th century glasses painted with figures and scenes in enamels, have survived. In gilded glass they can claim to have preceded the invention later known as *Zwischengoldglas* or *verre églomise*—gold leaf was laid on the surface of the glass, engraved with a fine point and then covered with another layer of glass. Portraits, some backed with blue glass, are known, but the most familiar are the Christian *fondi d'oro*, shallow bowls made for use in Christian burial ceremonies before the catacombs in Rome ceased to be used in A.D. 410. They have medallions in the centre, with Christian and even Jewish and classical subjects inscribed on gold leaf. The technique was also used in the Rhenish glass factories, especially Cologne, and a splendid large bowl is preserved in the British Museum, bearing scenes from the Old and New Testament in gilt, and blue, green and red enamels.

Most Roman glass has been recovered from the earth and since glass buried for any length of time, especially in damp soil, decays slightly on the surface, breaking up the light prismatically and producing an iridescent sheen, the pattern of the centuries gives an extraordinary lustre to the common pale green glass, which its mediaeval and Eastern successors lack. But even without this added beauty, Roman glassware reached a peak of almost fantastic refinement of form and colour and in such skills as gilding and overlay carving and cameo cutting. Then, after the 4th century A.D., continuing political and economic decay began to imperil the security and universality of the Empire. In the Middle East, continually subject to revolt and repression, glass making declined, but it was in the North, with the barbarian invasions, that the break with Roman tradition first occurred.

Islamic Glass
Splendid though the development of Islamic culture was, it had little impact on the state of decorative art in Western Europe in spite of (and perhaps because of) the Crusades. But towards the end of the Middle Ages, and especially with the import of Syrian wares, Islamic glass provided a standard which significantly influenced the Venetian manufacture and also stimulated a demand which, after the fall of Damascus in 1400, only Venice could sustain.

In the 8th and 9th centuries, as the glittering Caliphates of Bagdad, Egypt and Cordoba welded the South Mediterranean into an Islamic unity, glass makers revived the Alexandrian and Syrian traditions. Perhaps they merely continued them, because certain glasses which reached Europe in the 7th century and were called 'sapphire' or 'emerald' carvings, and lodged carefully in cathedral treasuries, were coloured glasses of Egyptian provenance. If Byzantium can be called the historical heir of Rome, it cannot be so described for some decorative arts, and glass manufacture in the declining remnants of the Empire after the 10th century reverted ultimately to the production of glazed mosaics. However, in the Southern Mediterranean, some of the techniques of Rome were actually surpassed and many were easily maintained. Cut and carved glass was made in the 9th and 10th centuries and overlay was attempted, although with less success than earlier at Alexandria. The colour of Islamic glass was rich and clear, and in Egypt a new art of lustre painting (whose composition is not yet fully understood) was achieved. The stains were sunk in some way through the surface of the glass, leaving no trace, and they therefore remained undimmed, unlike the Roman painting. Later, in the 12th century, Syrian glass makers took over, apparently from Egypt, the art of gilding and enamel painting, while in Southern Spain an indigenous Islamic tradition evolved which was to survive strongly in Andalusia into the 18th century.

Specimens reached Europe by devious routes, in the loot of crusading armies, or through Byzantium. To the relatively barbarous age of Charlemagne and the early Frankish kings, these glasses were a matter of wonder, rather like the fabulous elephant sent as a mark of favour to the Pope of the day by the great Caliph Haroun al Rashid. Some of them, beakers cut in high relief, were called *Hedwig* glasses and used as reliquaries in churches. Later, in the 13th and 14th centuries, as Europe underwent its progressive renaissance and as Italy, at least, opened rapidly to Byzantine and near Eastern influence, imports of Syrian enamelled glass increased steadily. Once thought to be Venetian, these glasses long pre-date manufacture at Murano and the fact that some are painted with Christian inscriptions may indicate that the designs were executed by artists at the Frankish court of Antioch or in Jerusalem after the third crusade. Painted in blue and red enamels, opaque white and gilt, these flasks and beakers were greatly prized in Europe, where they easily gave rise to legends such as that associated with the 'Luck of Eden Hall', a Syrian cup in a mediaeval leather case, probably brought back to Eden Hall in Westmorland by a crusading knight.

Two others in the British Museum, *c.* 1260, bear inscriptions in Latin 'dnia mater regis altissimi ora p. pa.' and 'magister aldrevandin (us) me fec (it)' suggesting that they are the work of an Italian living in Syria. There are several examples in Continental museums, notably in Dresden and Paris.

More imports came in during the 14th century, especially from Damascus. The famous mosque lamps of glass, with intricate enamel designs in Arabic lettering, were shipped from Egypt and Syria. Already, however, the Islamic world was facing the same danger which Rome had met in the barbarian invasions. Syrian glass shows a certain Asiatic influence in the period after the 1258 sack of Bagdad. Damascus was raided by the Mongol hordes in 1260 and 1300 and finally destroyed in 1400 by Tamerlane, who carried off the glass workers to Samarkand. Thereafter, Syrian exports declined rapidly. A few mosque lamps came to Europe in the 15th century, but apart from Spain, the art of fine glass making passed suddenly and irrevocably to the new factories of Venice.

Meanwhile, clinging to the traditions and vague memories of the art of Roman glass making, the forest glass works of Northern Europe had carried on in obscurity for 700 years, working out, not by imitation, but infinitely slow evolution, an idiom of their own. In many ways this vernacular work looked back to Rome, and that was certainly the intention of the glass workers, but in place of the universal trading community there was nothing but the most constricted regional demand. Hence the slow, painstaking need to overcome the lack of raw materials and the development of forms of glasses quite unknown to Rome. By the end of the Middle Ages, when the Venetian manufacturers set out to create and capture the market for fine glass, there already existed a tradition of glass making which could be called national in character and which in the 17th century was to break almost completely the dominance which Venice had acquired and then to last strongly until the age of mass production and beyond.

Mediæval European Coloured Glass and Early Vernacular Glass

All European glass dating from before the 17th century is rare and, if ever found outside museums, highly expensive. The illustrations in this volume therefore concentrate on the more recent centuries, apart from a few superb and rare examples. But the slow changes of the Middle Ages rank with the later conflict between indigenous styles and the Venetian manufacture as the important factors which determined national styles from the 17th to the 20th century.

The barbarian invasions, which eroded and finally destroyed the administrative and military machine of the Roman Empire, were not at first a total overthrow of civilisation. The first waves of Goths and Visigoths and even Vandals had lived near enough to the frontiers of the Empire to have absorbed some understanding of the Roman achievements, and this may explain why there was no radical decline in glass making. The skills are largely taught by example and it was, perhaps, migration as the tribes moved from Germany across Gaul and Spain and down to North Africa, which broke up the tradition of fine glass making. The demand had ceased by the end of the 6th century and only the manufacture in common green glass of vessels for household use continued. Gradually, even such relatively simple skills as joining a foot to the body of a glass ceased to be practised.

In what may be called the Teutonic or Merovingian period, from the 6th to the 11th centuries, glass followed a few simple forms chiefly used for drinking. Lack of skill and the fact that in the use to which they were put, glasses were probably taken and refilled as soon as they were empty, explains the characteristic Seine–Rhine beaker, conical in shape, usually decorated with trailed ornament or threads of differently coloured glass (see pp. 20–21 in the previous volume). These, and the few bowls and cups without handles which survive, are made mainly of bubbly green metal, but deep greens, browns and ambers are known. No distinctive traits show the difference between the Seine and Rhine area and while there may have been an export trade to the north, it is also possible that they were made in Britain as well. At the end of the 7th century, the Abbot of Wearmouth in Durham, almost the only remaining civilised part of England, wrote asking for glass makers to be sent from Gaul.

So little is known of the first half of the Middle Ages that it is not easy to discern trends. There is documentary evidence that the skills of Rome were handed down: the processes of glass making described by Pliny were repeated by monastic writers such as Hrabanus Maurus in his *De Universo*: but there is no evidence that they were put into use and, by mere repetition, accuracy tended to diminish. The monk Theophilus of Paderborn in Westphalia, however, in his *Schedula Diversarum Artium* gave a tolerable treatise on the subject.

The fact that the chief supplies of soda were cut off by the disruption of trade with Spain and North Africa forced the forest glass makers to rely wholly on potash, an inferior substance. Given only their own ingenuity and the requirements of a small localised market, the Seine–Rhine

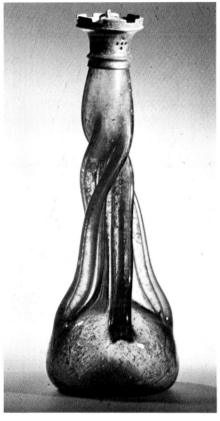

area did however produce new forms—curved drinking horns and a drinking glass known as a *Russelbecher*, tall and funnel shaped, with applied drops of glass, drawn out like the drooping trunks of elephants, all round the side.

Few examples survive, presumably because of the high rate of breakage; and it is clear that, by contrast with the work done for the church, the only great patron of the time, domestic glass making, even in the 12th century, was a very minor art indeed. Artistry went into stained glass, made by itinerant glass blowers, like the wandering masons who helped build the great gothic cathedrals of France and Germany. During the 13th and 14th centuries the position began to change and in the 15th century glass making entered on a new stage, both in quantity and quality. The secular growth of the Holy Roman Empire and of the national state of France, the decline in political authority of the Papacy and, above all, the increase in volume of trade along the great routes across Europe inspired a new demand.

In Germany in the *Waldglas* period of the later Middle Ages, few advances were made on the Teutonic period until after 1400 but the number of glass houses seems to have increased in Hesse, around Cologne, in Bavaria, and on the mountainous wooded borders of Bohemia and Silesia. There, production concentrated on phials, flasks and articles for alchemists and apothecaries (one of the earliest manuscript drawings to show a glass vessel is of a doctor examining a specimen bottle). New forms appeared in the 15th century, first the rare *Maigelein*, a beaker with its base pushed in, with a high domed kick, and moulded with a design around the side. The most notable development, and one which influenced glass making for at least 200 years, was the *Römer*, a goblet decorated with applied blobs of glass on the stem. These are distinct from the earlier *Russelbecher*, because the drops are not hollow, although in the case of the *Krautstrunk* (cabbage stem) goblets, *Warzenbecker* or *Nuppenbecher*, they are drawn out to a point. In the first stage, *Römers* were cylindrical or conical in shape, with the drops around the lower part, but gradually the lip of the glass was developed into the bowl of the typical *Römer* of the 16th century.

As the *Römer* acquired a distinct stem, the foot was formed by winding a glass thread closely around a core of wood or metal; later the foot was blown like the bowl and the thread laid on top of it, as in later examples. The drops on the stem, called prunts by English glass makers, came to be decorated with a pattern like a raspberry, or more rarely with moulded masks. The colour of *Römers* tends to deepen, so that the green in 16th century examples is a fine rich metal; the form became so popular that it was exported all over Europe and survived through the 19th century as a glass for hock, down to the present day. But the period in which *Römers* reached their most noble proportions and colour was the 17th century, when their manufacture spread also to Belgium and the Netherlands.

Despite its later popularity, the *Römer* was essentially a mediaeval type of glass, the highest development of indigenous German style. So were the rarer large *Römers* with elaborately moulded covers, and the *Daumenglas*, with its inserted hollows for fingers to hold the body. Other shapes seem rather to have been a response to the effect of Venetian competition in the early 16th century. The *Kuttrolf* was a type of bottle made with several intertwined necks, joined in a large and irregular mouth, which was used apparently for slow pouring or drinking, like the contemporary Spanish

Three *Römers*, one without prunts, *c.* 1650, the others with flat raspberry prunts, *c.* 1660, and with raised raspberry prunts, *c.* 1675.
Low Countries.
4¼, 5¼ and 4⅞ in. high.

Howard Phillips

A jug with onion-shaped body, flared opening, two bands about the neck, swan-necked spout and handle.
Low Countries, mid-17th century.
5⅝ in. high.

Howard Phillips

porro. The *Igel* (hedgehog) glass was club-shaped with prunts like the spines of a hedgehog. The decadent, often cruel, taste of the waning Middle Ages inclined to fantasy—to puzzle glasses for drinking feats or practical jokes, and to weird animal shaped vessels, boots, hats and barrels, nearly all of which are in greens, browns or yellows.

A distinct form of very tall cylindrical beaker with a foot akin to that of the *Römer*, was called *Stangenglas* (pole glass). Made at first in *Waldglas* in the Lower Rhine, it later became the only generic form successfully to adapt to the clear Venetian metal in the 16th century. When divided by thin trails of glass into equal parts, these tall beakers are called *Passglas* since they were handed round the table so that each guest could drink down to the next line. Some *Stangenglas* are of vast size. In the 17th century smaller heavier examples became known as *Humpen* and were then the basis for the German art of enamelling.

In the later Middle Ages, German workmen followed the trade routes north to Liège, Antwerp and even Scandinavia. From Saxony and Bohemia into Lorraine there was no great difference in the style or type of glass they produced. But in France two different methods of producing flat glass of some size evolved. The Broad or Lorraine method was to blow a long cylinder of glass, cut it open on one side, then roll it flat; in Normandy the glass makers used the Crown method which involved spinning the pontil rod until the glass batch widened into a flat plate with a bull's eye in the centre. Both these methods were employed to make window glass in the 15th and 16th century, while in Lorraine, from much earlier, a manufacture of crude mirror glass existed. Backed with lead or silver, these mirrors were usually held by carved ivory frames of Gothic style.

In mediaeval France, however, apart from the export of window glass, stained glass manufacture was supreme. The greenish *verre de fougère*, similar to the *Waldglas* of Germany, was simple and failed to develop the vernacular exhuberance of the *Römer* or *Stangenglas*. In Spain, on the other hand, the Gothic period gave rise to a remarkable efflorescence of styles and colours. Under the first Visigothic invaders, the Roman tradition was maintained [1] in green glass and the use of coloured glass like jewels set in metals or *cloisonné* work. Under the Caliphate of Cordoba, most glass seems to have been imported from Syria and Egypt, but by the 11th century, when the Caliphate was in decline, a style, part Moorish and part native, reached vigorous maturity in Andalusia. Centred on the cities of Almeria, Murcia, Malaga, Seville and Granada, Southern Spain remained a largely closed community for 400 years until the reconquest by the Catholic Spanish kings, who extended the protection of the glass industry until the time of Charles V and the incursion of Venice.

Spain, of course, had her own supply of the finest soda, the *barilla*, made in the salt marshes on the Mediterranean coast. The early mediaeval Andalusian wares underwent little change in style even to the 18th century and this lack of innovation and the naïve domestic nature of the products probably explains why after the reconquest, manufacture was re-established in Catalonia and centred on the great trading city of Barcelona. Here, in the monasteries of the Pyrenean foothills, like Poblet, where glass making was established in the 12th century, and along the coast to Perpignan, which was not then culturally part of France, glass making flourished. Few examples of the Gothic age before 1500 survive, but manuscript drawings and inventories show that even in the 14th century there was an export trade and that the main objects were wine cups and globe-shaped flasks, with long necks, in green and brown. Much was imported from Syria (*Vidre de Damas*) and some vessels, such as the rose water sprinkler or *Almorratxa*, later a familiar form, may have been made specially for the Spanish market. Copies of Syrian enamelled glasses were made and by the 15th century factories existed all round Barcelona and as far along the coast as Tarragona and Valencia. Inland, in Castille, was the factory at Cadalso de los Vidrios. At the peak of Gothic style, Spanish glass in blue, purple, yellow, with some examples in clear glass was probably the foremost in Europe. As far as can be gauged, most Catalan glass was enamelled in Mudejar pattern, half Moorish, half Spanish, stylised and quite unlike the naturalistic painting of contemporary Venice. By 1500 Spain, united under the Catholic kings, rich already and soon to be master of the New World, possessed the only glass manufacture in Europe able to challenge the Venetian competition.

Venetian Glass

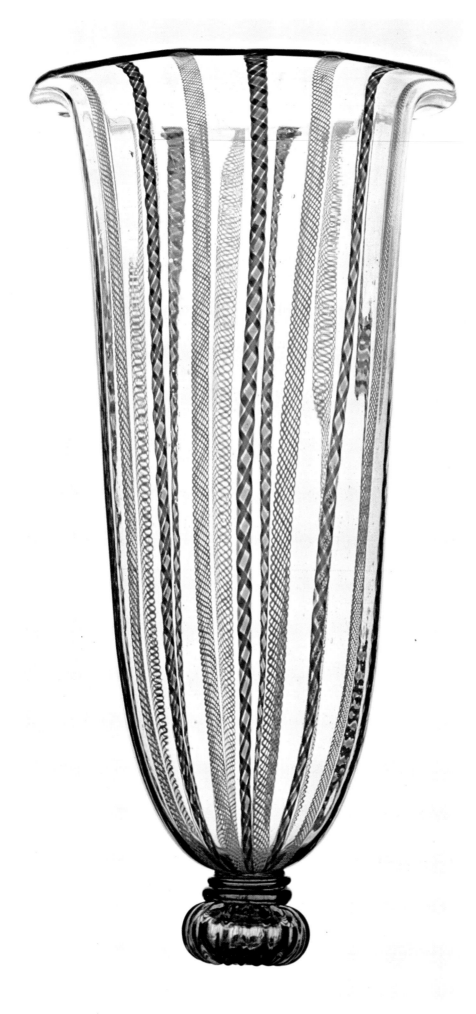

Almost in the lifetime of a single glass blower in the 16th century, Venice captured the European market in decorative glass ware. Although there is no knowledge of glass making in the islands of Venice before the 11th century, it is almost certain that the Roman traditions survived. At Ravenna, the Byzantine Empire lasted until the 8th century and glazed tiles were produced for the great mosaics of the churches. The earliest Venetian articles were probably very simple in comparison with those of Syria; small objects, mirrors and window glass. By the 13th century, when Venice was the largest Christian trading city in the Mediterranean, glass making was well established and had been almost wholly transferred to the smaller island of Murano because of the dangers of fire to the crowded houses from the furnaces. According to the chronicle of Martino da Canale (1260) glass vessels of some size were common. A hundred years later, glass was being exported from Venice to Spain, to other towns in Italy and northwards across the Brenner Pass over the Alps into Germany.

Venice possessed almost unrivalled advantages for the export of glass after the fall of Damascus ended the Syrian art. Her geographical position, wealth and trading skill, and the careful diplomacy which the Doges and their ambassadors pursued, kept the republic largely free from war and invasion. With the greatest fleet in the Mediterranean, she could evade the worst of the Turkish and Algerian pirates. With the inherited skills and traditions of glass making only luck was needed; and luck came with the discovery of the use of manganese as the first efficient decolourising agent, and with the fashionable demand for clear glass which swept the rest of Europe in the 16th century.

Clear Venetian glass, the *cristallo*, was perfected by 1500. Fine coloured glass, chiefly of deep blue, was rediscovered in the same period and although used at first in typical mediaeval style to simulate precious stones, it was being fashioned into substantial goblets by the end of the 15th century. Venetian commercial shrewdness demanded a closed manufacture and for 200 years the Republic attempted to maintain an elaborate monopoly, legislating strictly for a guild organisation, with high penalties for workmen who betrayed the secrets of the art or who escaped to sell their knowledge on the mainland. Even the export of materials, the silica obtained from the quartz pebbles of the river Ticino, or the soda ash from Spain, was prohibited, as was that of cullet, the broken fragments of glass which could be melted down and used again.

In spite of such restrictions, factories were established at Bologna and Ferrara, and existed in many areas of Italy by the 16th century. The main competition, however, came from L'Altare, a town near Genoa where forest glass workers from Normandy had settled. After 1450, backed by the commercial strength of Genoa, the Altarists, as they were called, began to expand elsewhere. Unlike the Venetians, they refused to maintain a secret monopoly and it is more than likely that their almost modern practice of setting up glass manufacture inside the frontiers of European countries, forced the Venetians to do the same. The glass made by immigrant Italian workers is almost indistinguishable from the products of Venice and Altare, and is referred to in the next chapter.

The Venetian *cristallo*, still bearing traces of colour in a faint smoky brown or yellow, fused easily and quickly and could be manipulated into delicate and elaborate shapes. But the most celebrated of Venetian forms, the intricately twisted stems, belong to the late 16th and 17th century and to the period of the Italian factories in the Netherlands, Germany, France and Spain. In the earlier days, when a certain mediaeval flavour still characterised the work, Venetian glass was mainly coloured and decorated in enamels, in typical renaissance style.

Local tradition has always ascribed the invention or rediscovery of painting in enamel colours, which were then fused in the heat of the furnace, to Angelo Barovier, a Venetian glass maker. In fact, the technique is almost identical with that used in Syria where Italian workmen were trained at the end of the Middle Ages, but most of the very early vessels of punch bowl type in deep blue glass, painted with portraits or

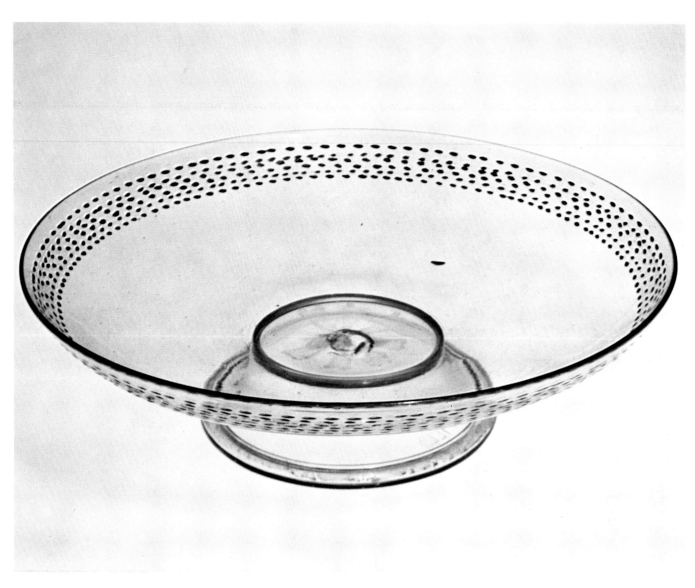

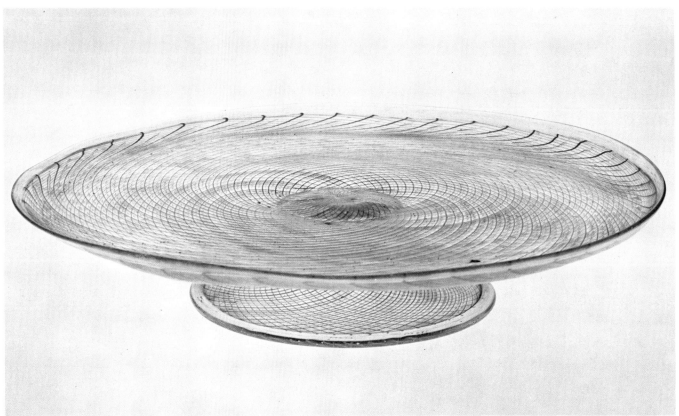

A Tazza with polychrome decoration in the form of dots, and gilding.
Venice, mid-16th century.
9¼ in. diameter.

Richard Dennis

A vase decorated with *latticino* work.
Venice, mid-17th century.
7 in. high.

Leslie Scott

processions, usually to celebrate the weddings of the nobility, are still ascribed to 'Barovier'. Like all very early Venetian glass ware, these few examples are of the greatest rarity. Other, rather taller, azure blue goblets on wrought and knopped stems, had classical and allegorical scenes. Vessels in green and purple glass are also known and some of the unpainted goblets are engraved with a diamond point, a technique much more popular at the Italian factory in Hall in Tyrol, but in which a number of glasses were made in Venice in the 16th century.

The earliest surviving clear glass vessels, painted in the same palette of blue, green, yellow, red and white, date from just before 1500. A magnificent flask in the Civic Museum of Bologna bears two coats of arms to celebrate the wedding of Ginevra Sforza and Giovanni Bentivoglio in 1492. Enamel paintings, portraits, figures and coats of arms in the centre of glass plates from Murano date from the same period; all are well executed in the fashion of the last quarter of the late 15th century. Jugs, dishes, tazzas, in clear or blue glass are known and also the first of the vessels known as *cesendelli*, hanging lamps for use in churches. *Vetro cal-*

Bottom — Left
A Tazza with *latticino* decoration.
Venice, probably mid-17th century.

Leslie Scott

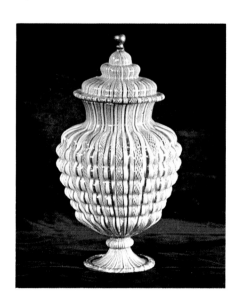

Top—left
A ewer with *latticino* decoration.
Probably Venice, early 17th century.
Corning Museum

Right
A bowl in marbled jasper glass *(Schmelzglas)*.
Venice, early 16th century.
9 in. diameter.
Sotheby & Co.

Bottom left
A *vetro di trina* goblet.
Probably Venice, early 17th century.
Corning Museum

Right
A covered vase, mould-blown, with *latticino* decoration.
Venice or the Low Countries, late 16th or early 17th century.
Corning Museum

A standing bowl with applied blue threading.
Venice, *c.* 1600.
10½ in. diameter.

Richard Dennis

cedonio, a form of marbled coloured glass imitating chalcedony, onyx or agate, and sometimes called *Schmelzglas*, was made up to the end of the 16th century in the simple early shapes.

The 16th century was the greatest age of Venetian craftsmanship. The massive quality of the early pieces, still reminiscent of silver flagons and dishes, gave way to smaller more flexible compositions, whose lightness matched the thin hard metal of the clear *cristallo*. Trailing work was imprinted on the glass with pincers and drops in the form of masks and lion's heads; and handles and stems of glasses began to be worked in more elaborate ways. By the mid-16th century coloured glass fell into disuse, being replaced almost entirely by clear glass, plain or decorated in enamel, or worked in white and coloured threads to make the well known *latticino* designs. The *cristallo* was unsuitable for ponderous work in thick enamel paint and the typical bowls, cups with covers, plates, ewers and wine flasks of Murano are decorated with bands and patterns of different coloured dots, with lines of soft gilding. Rims were frequently in blue glass. Many of the finer examples bear coats of arms or heraldic emblems, exquisitely painted; but some of these are suspect since the addition of unfired painting presents no great difficulty to the forger.

Even this form of painting began to decline before 1600, except for glasses made for foreign orders, and 17th century pieces tend to be only lightly decorated with dots or occasionally gilding alone. For a short time a class of extremely rare dishes was painted in unfired oil colours in genre subjects or copies of canvases by Raphael and other masters. Bearing delicate and fine gilt scroll work and being very susceptible to damage, they were presumably made to order purely for decoration.

Another form of glass dating from the 15th century is that called variously *latticino*, *lattimo*, or later in Germany, *milchglas*. When Chinese porcelain first became known in Europe, attempts were made to copy it in opaque white glass made by adding tin oxide or arsenic to the mixture of ingredients. The first record of this occurs in about 1470, although few examples are known to date from before 1500. *Milchglas* offered an admirable surface for the work of the enameller and this may explain its popularity in Venice down to the 18th century. Early cups, goblets and

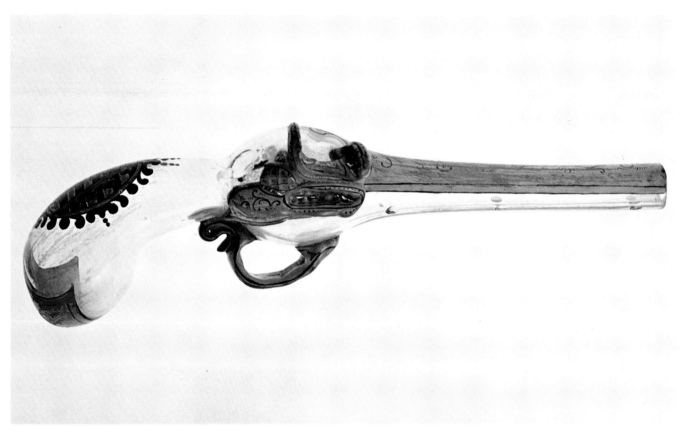

A glass pistol with armorial painting.
Venice or Bohemia, *c.* 1750.
9 in. long.

Sotheby & Co.

chalices were decorated with figure painting, like the blue Barovier pieces, in the style of the Venetian artist Vittore Carpaccio, or in copies of the contemporary maiolica ware. So-called pilgrim flasks were particularly suitable for this type of painting because of the large surface offered by each side of the body.

Opaque white threads had been used by the Romans to produce spiral patterns in their glass and this art was revived about 1530 to produce the most characteristic Venetian style. Called *latticino* work, the patterns were made by inserting the opaque glass rods into a gathering of clear glass, twisting and manipulating it to produce the required curved or interlaced pattern and then blowing it as usual. The most delicate spirals made a pattern as fine as lace and was therefore called *vetro di trina*. *Latticino* work showed to best advantage on large surfaces and was used on plates, beakers, covered cups, all of considerable size; and it also formed a large part of the *façon de Venise* production outside Italy. Some later designs included coloured threads and broad bands of opaque white, with thin *latticino* in between. The fashion continued undiminished into the 19th century and because the earlier designs were continually copied, examples are often impossible to date with accuracy.

Last of the Venetian innovations (although this also had origins in antiquity) was the *millefiori* technique. Bundles of rods of different colours made up to represent small stylised flowers were embedded in clear glass. A very early Murano bowl of this type with scalloped edges is in the Victoria and Albert Museum. Aventurine glass, a 17th century technique, was not dissimilar. A mixture of copper oxide and forge scales was added to the molten glass, which created particles of clear copper and gave a bizarre effect, rather like a dress of polished sequins.

Lattimo plate with a view of the Church of the Carita in red.
Venice, *c.* 1741, probably made at the Miotti Glasshouse.

Corning Museum

The 17th century was distinguished for the adventurous inspiration of the glass blower, rather than new forms of decoration. Enamelling dropped almost entirely out of favour and was replaced by the addition of handles, stems, rims or feet of coloured glass, to a clear body. At the same time the forms of the vessels changed, becoming even lighter, and, in the manipulation of stems, handles and finials, almost fantastic. Glasses and covered cups were elongated, their rims wrought into deep waves and gadroons, and in the stems of wine glasses imagination ran wild, giving rise to convoluted serpents, and elaborate tiers of baluster knops with threaded and looped supports. In the Netherlands, fashion took the style even further, while Venetians also derived a series of conceits in the form of animals, fish, fruit and even ships, most of which could, with care, be used for drinking.

The power and influence of the Venetian Republic declined steadily through the 18th century until its eventual extinction by Napoleon. Whether influenced by the changed nature of their position in the world or not, the glass makers continued to repeat the fashions and styles of the earlier periods of the great tradition. *Latticino* work showed virtually no change from the 16th century, although it was distinguished for a period in the 18th in the glass house of Guiseppe Riati. The main development lay in the vogue for opaque white plates, decorated with scenes and landscapes of Venice. A set of plates painted after Canaletto, in red, was brought back to England by Horace Walpole in 1741. They were a speciality of the glass factory of the Miotti family. Other designs copied those on imported Chinese porcelain, the landscapes of 18th century maiolica, and the *Hausmaler* painting of Meissen. Opaque white was also used as a base for marbled 'calcedonio' work, not unlike the 16th century examples.

In general, 18th century Venetian glass making degenerated into a trivial and repetitive manufacture and the painting on clear glass which was resumed was crude and unsatisfactory. Some gilt and faceted bottles and decanters were produced of a type indistinguishable from the Spanish factory of La Granja. The best work seems to have gone into engraved glass in a desperate attempt to counter the competition from Bohemia, but the thin Venetian *cristallo* was unsuitable for the cutting and in spite of the ten-year privilege given to Briati in 1736 the productions lacked the dignity of the deep cut glasses of Germany. Already Murano was a tourist centre and a good deal of energy went into fanciful toys, not unlike the later products of Bristol and Nailsea—pistols, trumpets and a host of small animals, some in clear glass, some in *latticino*. Associated with the demand for trinkets, the manufacture of artificial pearls was carried on, particularly by the Miotti glass works. Coloured beads and jet were well-known—'it is with artificial jet, cut and pierced and threaded with silk thread, that embroideries are made in sufficiently good taste, but very dear, which are used particularly in churches', one English traveller noted. Another fashion was that of chevron beads, made in the form of cylinders with rounded ends, out of layers of coloured glass divided by sections of opaque white.

Venetian mirrors had been famous all over Europe from the 16th century, and remained in demand even after the invention of plate glass casting in France. In the 18th century they were frequently engraved and a large export of mirror frames, heavily swathed in coloured flowers, was maintained. Similar in style were the great many-branched rococo chandeliers, in which pinks and opaque whites predominated. Smaller copies of these were made right through the 19th century.

The period of decadence lasted until the 1860s and the classical revival associated with Antonio Salviati. Having suffered the critical loss of the European market to national competition in the later 17th century, Venetian glass makers turned inwards irrevocably and failed to respond even to the remarkable wave of inspiration which overflowed Germany in the first half of the 19th century—an illustration perhaps of how closely the domestic art is tied to the demands and tastes of the market place.

Façon de Venise

Italian domination of the trade in fine glass lasted from about 1500 to the third quarter of the 17th century in Spain, Germany and Britain and rather longer in the Netherlands and France. Production falls into two categories: those glasses made in Venice for export, chiefly to specific orders; and that of factories set up by emigrant Italian masters in the various countries of Europe. Because of the similarity of Venetian and Altarist workmanship there is virtually no difference between glasses made in Italy and those elsewhere, called *façon de Venise*, so that in many cases the only means of differentiation lies in certain regional styles and characteristics.

Venetian exports have been traced mainly from documentary evidence such as the orders placed by the London glass works of John Greene with Alessio Morelli of Murano between 1667 and 1673, at a time before George Ravenscroft had discovered his famous English glass of lead. Drawings of these glasses are preserved in the British Museum and show among others the typical trumpet shaped *façon de Venise* wine glasses. Somewhat

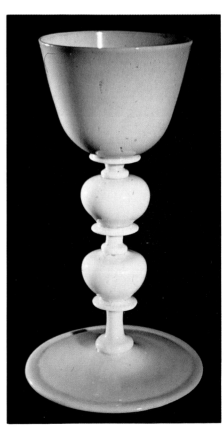

Left
Façon de Venise beaker with *latticino* and coloured threads, on three feet.
Probably Low Countries, first half of the 17th century.
3½ in. high.   *Sotheby & Co.*

Below
An opaque white goblet.
Liège, 17th century.   *Corning Museum*

earlier, glasses decorated in enamels with coats of arms were supplied for German noble families. Several of these bear dates of the first two decades of the 16th century and were formerly thought to have been made in Nuremberg. As late as the early 18th century, *latticino* goblets, some of fantastic shapes, and vessels of deep blue coloured glass, were supplied to the Rosenborg Palace in Copenhagen for Frederick IV of Denmark. Probably the largest quantity of glass exported was, however, that of mirror plates, mirror frames, and in the 18th century, chandeliers. About the year 1500, Venetian craftsmen had learned to make flat sheets of glass by the Lorraine cylinder method and soon set up a separate corporation to manufacture mirror glass. Thereafter, until the invention of cast plate glass in Normandy at the end of the 17th century, they held virtually the whole of the European market.

The transplanting of Italian industry over Europe was a remarkable phenomenon, greatly assisted by the political unification achieved by the Holy Roman Empire under Charles V. Austria, large areas of Germany including Bohemia and Silesia, Spain and the Netherlands, Milan and

Two *façon de Venise* wine glasses with winged stems.
Venice or the Netherlands, *c.* 1640.
8 and 8½ in. high.

Leslie Scott

A *façon de Venise* style beaker.
Germany or the Netherlands.

Leslie Scott

Naples, all came under the authority of the Hapsburg monarchy and,
despite the turbulence of the Reformation and the war with the Netherlands, Europe assumed an aspect which it had not possessed since the late
Roman Empire. Within what was virtually a super-state, some of the
difficulties which had impeded trade in the late Middle Ages disappeared.
Sea and river transport improved considerably and the burdens of tolls
and customs at the frontiers of petty German states were rationalised in
favour of the glass trade by princes who had every interest in the enlarge-
ment of what was, in many cases, their principal industry. The vast
quantity of glass ware made in the German factories in the 17th century
is referred to later—that of *façon de Venise* glass ware, being finer and more
delicately wrought, was not so great, but still sufficient for it to be considered
a major item in domestic trade.

Some of the earliest factories were established by workmen who wished
to escape from the elaborate regulations of the Venetian state monopoly,
but the Altarists were subject to no such restriction and were presumably
sensitive to the great commercial advantage of working inside the national
frontiers of their customers. Glass making had already become a profession,
carrying a status similar to that of goldsmith or silversmith, and craftsmen
were eagerly seized on, enticed away from competitors and given privileges
or monopolies. Jacob Verzelini, for example, was awarded a privilege
in London by Queen Elizabeth in 1575. A French historian has written
that 'en France on restait noble quoique l'on fût verrier, qu'a Venise on
était noble parce que l'on était verrier, et qu'a Altare on n'était verrier que
parce que l'on etait noble'.[1] The immigrant manufacturers guarded their
art with care, but they had to train pupils and workmen, and so from the

[1]Quoted in W. B. Honey, *Glass* (London,
1942), p. 137. In France one remained
noble in spite of being a glass maker; in
Venice one was noble because one was a
glass maker; and in Altare one could only
be a glass maker if one was noble.

30

centres of Hall in Tyrol, Antwerp, Liège, Nuremberg, Barcelona and many smaller glass houses in Germany, France and Britain, there spread out local works which grew steadily over the next 150 years.

Of these, Hall in Tyrol and the Netherlands tended to specialise in coloured glass. Antonio Neri, writing *L'Arte Vetraria* in 1612, gave the formula for the different colours used in Antwerp where workmen from Murano had arrived as early as 1541. The Liège glass works, later controlled by the French family of Bonhomme, was founded by Altarists about 1569 and developed a subsidiary house at Maastricht, as Antwerp had at Amsterdam and Middleburg. Much of the *façon de Venise* glass ware of the Low Countries is similar to Venetian work but there is also a distinctive elongation of forms, particularly in *latticino* glass. Immensely tall and thin trumpet-shaped goblets with covers in *vetro di trina* are associated with the Netherlands; and beakers and goblets in *latticino* with applied masks, often gilded and enamelled, can be ascribed to Liège. Tankards, unknown in Venice, are found with lids and mounts in silver or pewter, and in vessels made for pouring, the spout tends to be long and sinuous like those of Catalonia. The most characteristic forms of this region are the serpent glasses ('Coppen mit Serpenten', as the Venetian, Nicholas Stua, described them in 1667), wine glasses with elaborately wrought openwork stems, carrying twin coloured serpents on the outside and again on the cover. Other stems bear pronounced wings. Where these resemble a double-headed eagle the glasses are usually called German. Sometimes the stems have multi-coloured threads drawn through them. Ice glass, formed by rapidly cooling and reheating the glass to give a frosted crackled appearance, was also made at Liège. In general, all Low Countries' *façon de Venise* work is less graceful than the Italian original, betraying perhaps the temper of the local workmen, or the less elegant taste of the customer.

A factory was set up at Hall in Tyrol in 1534, and grew to considerable importance, first under the direction of Sebastian Hochstetter in the late 16th century and afterwards under the patronage of the Hapsburgs. Midway between Vienna, Venice and the trade route to Germany via Augsberg, Hall was ideally situated. As well as clear glass, *façon de Venise*, Hall produced a quantity of superb dark green and blue glass, chiefly in the form of large cylindrical goblets and vases with covers, the stems

31

Scherzpokal, or trick glass, decorated with hollow-blown half figures of a stag and a bridled horse.
German, mid-17th century.
11 in. high.

Sotheby & Co.

and finials of which were profusely knopped. Most of them are decorated in diamond point engraving, with lacquer painting and gilding in unfired oils on the clear specimens.

[2]Honey, op. cit., p. 64.

According to Honey[2] the diamond point engraving on glasses of the late 16th century from Nuremberg, Saxony, Holland, Vienna and also those attributed to Verzelini in London, is very similar to the Hall technique, suggesting that workmen had been lured from there to foreign capitals. Certainly the technique spread rapidly in Holland in the 17th and 18th centuries where it was applied to decanters of the *Heemskirk* type and winged stem *façon de Venise* glasses with coloured bowls. In Nuremberg, Silesia and Bohemia, coloured glasses engraved with coats of arms were fashionable until the end of the 17th century.

Other German glass in *façon de Venise* is hard to identify. Italian crafts-men worked at Cassel and *latticino* glass was made in Saxony, Silesia and Bohemia into the 17th century, with a distinct class of beakers enamelled with Saxon coats of arms. Various *Stangen* glasses enamelled with figures (a pair, one of which bears the name of Jakob Praun and his wife, are in the British Museum) or coats of arms with dates may be ascribed to Italian workmen, but the strong tradition of German enamelled glass described in the next chapter makes this a matter of rather academic definition. English glass of this period was described in the previous volume and it is only necessary to repeat here that one of the goblets associated with Verzelini is of purple glass.

In France it seems possible that the Venetians and Altarists who arrived during the late 15th century found little competition from the vernacular glass works. Ravaged by the wars with England, France had declined as a centre of glass making. A privilege granted in 1338, however, indicates the very remarkable quantity of glass ware which the French houses had been able to produce in the late Middle Ages—something which, even for the Royal Court, would be incredible if it were not partly confirmed by later accounts from Germany. 'The Dauphin resigns to Guionet a part of the forest of Chambarant in order that he may establish a glass manu-facture there on condition that the latter supply annually for his own house 100 dozen glasses in the form of bells, 12 dozen small glasses with wide tops, 20 dozen goblets and cups with feet, 12 amphorae, 36 dozen chamber pots, 12 large decanters, 6 dishes, 6 dishes without edges, 12 pots, 12 ewers, etc. etc.', a vast collection, including lamps.

Of all this and the copious *façon de Venise* work which followed in the 16th and 17th centuries, very few examples survive which can be classed as French with any degree of certainty—an indication also of the high rate of breakage at what were presumably uninhibited banquets and entertainments. One of the earliest French pieces, a dish enamelled with the arms of Louis XIII and Anne of Britanny, is in the Musée de Cluny, together with a later goblet showing a minister of the court of Henry II and his wife. Some of them are painted with figures and inscriptions, with a type of scroll work between horizontal bands of gilding and enamel dots, which is not found outside France. The best known glass works was founded by Theseo Mutio, an Altarist, at St Germain en Laye in 1551. Other fac-tories are known to have existed in Poitou, Normandy and Provence, in fact in the areas where the forest supplied almost unlimited quantities of wood for the furnaces. Some marbled glass in bright colours, usually on a pale blue ground, not unlike the *Schmelzglas* of Venice, has always been attributed to France: bottles, pilgrim flasks and vessels of barrel shape are so described.

The Italians met the strongest competition in Spain, and in Barcelona, where the Islamic and Gothic traditions lasted strongly until the 16th century, a curious and vigorous blend of styles emerged as a result. The policy of protection of the glass trade which helped to stimulate Catalan manufacture was maintained until the accession of the Emperor Charles V. Then Spain became part of the Holy Roman Empire and the industry opened into the ambit of the Italians, chiefly by imports from Antwerp, in Hapsburg Flanders, which were much cheaper than those of Venice. To this stimulus, the glass blowers of Catalonia responded with a skill which

Spaniards at least believed to surpass that of the originals. 'The glass that today is made in Venice is considered excellent, but in many ways that made in Barcelona is better . . . and so Catalonia is praised and esteemed for its glass and boxes (of it) are shipped to Castilla, the West Indies, France and elsewhere.'[3]

In the early 16th century, Barcelona produced blue, purple and less often green glass, opaque white and combinations of two colours; also clear glasses with coloured feet and handles. *Vetro calcedonio* and marble glass like that of France was known and vessels with speckled gold like aventurine. Except for armorial designs, paintings still drew on mudejar motifs, unlike those of Venice. Animals, birds, a few human figures and angels appear with religious inscriptions. Other designs were composed of dots of enamel, simulating jewels or pearls, and a fish scale pattern reminiscent of early Venetian work.

Some idea of the quantity produced is indicated by the fact that Ferdinand of Aragon gave his Queen Isabella 148 glasses as a present in 1503: to the normal plates, bowls, jugs, covered goblets, ewers, flasks and wine glasses of the inventory, may be added altar candlesticks and the peculiarly Spanish rose-water sprinkler—a vase-shaped vessel with several spouts, called an *almorratxa*.

In the mid-16th century, Italian workmen penetrated Spain. They settled chiefly in Castille where there was less competition, but some taught the Venetian skills in Catalonia. Among them, a member of the famous Barovier family was working in Majorca in 1600 and later at El Escorial, the palace of Philip II near Madrid. The fashion for clear crystal over-rode the earlier coloured glass of Barcelona and for almost two hundred years after 1550, the Catalans turned to brilliantly enamelled imitations of Venetian forms. Very few of these glasses survive. All are made of a faintly yellow or grey metal, thick enough to stand the firing of the painting. 'Crystal glasses when completely finished are painted with green, gold and other colours, and returned to the furnace for annealing; and that colouring remains so fixed that it can be rarely, if ever, separated' wrote a contemporary historian.[4] Unlike Venetian examples, however, the artists covered the whole body of the glass with arabesques of trees, leaves, flowers and birds, and occasional diminutive figures, so that the effect is not unlike that of Persian miniature painting. Some show hunts with hounds in pursuit of stags, or the insignia of religious orders like the Knights of Malta or the Jesuits.

Diamond point engraving was employed later in the 16th century, together with the use of *latticino*. In Spain the opaque white rods were less delicate than the lace work of Venice and appear as solid bands, twisted and looped in bold designs. Many of the Catalan vessels have prunts gilded in enamel like those of Liège in Spanish Flanders. The versatility of the glass blower was shown in the design of wine glasses, not as in the Low Countries, in elaborate stems and finials, but in flared and patterned bowls and in the glass toys and animals which made Barcelona as much as a 17th century tourist paradise as Venice itself. Polychrome ornaments, glass jewels, buttons, rings and chains were what caught the eye of an Italian traveller in 1664: 'In this city of Barcelona the glass trinkets are most admirable'.

The *façon de Venise* lasted in Catalonia until the rapid political and economic decline of Spain in the mid-17th century and also in Seville (whence it was exported, with numerous glass workers, to Mexico and Peru). Cadalso near Toledo was another centre, producing mainly domestic glass in the 16th century, but later good copies of Venetian work, especially *latticino*. Refreshed by an influx of Italians from Flanders, the style survived here rather longer than elsewhere, but had decayed by 1700 when the demands of the Spanish Court fashion turned irrevocably away from the thin *cristallo* to heavier glass, wheel engraved and gilt in the French manner. There was no Spanish revolt against the Venetian style as in Germany and England. When the finest glass of Catalonia ceased to be made, the workers reverted to traditional Spanish forms, while in the south, the

[3]Père Gil, a 16th century Catalan priest. Quoted in A. W. Frothingham, *Spanish Glass* (New York, 1964), p. 30.

[4]Quoted in Frothingham, op. cit., p. 37.

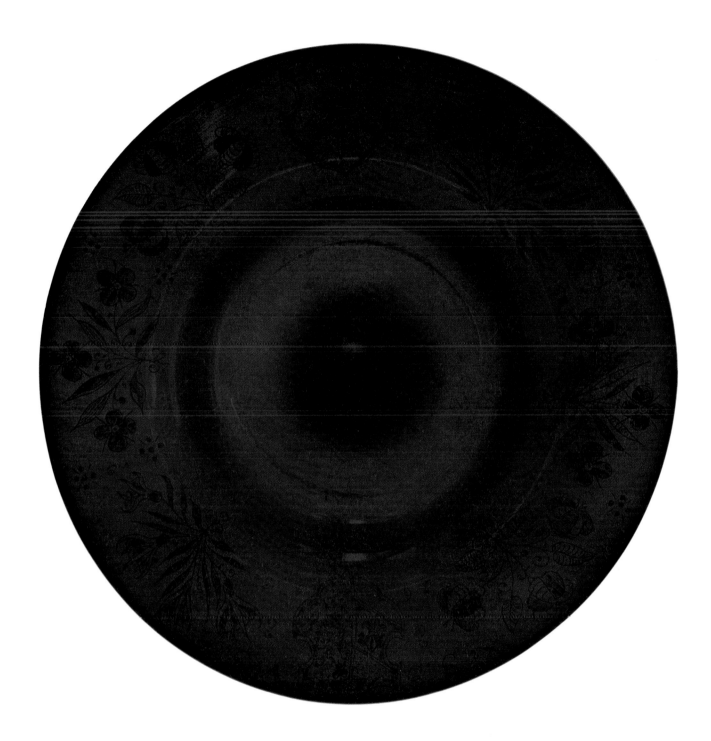

A very rare German purple glass plate, dated 1613, engraved in the diamond point with armorial designs to commemorate a marriage between two Saxon families, von Berbisdorf and Schato von Schatental. 9½ in. diameter.

Sotheby & Co.

Over page
Façon de Venise pilgrim flask.
Spain, probably Barcelona, early 16th century style.
11 in. high.

Leslie Scott

vernacular Moorish styles revived with astonishing vigour.

Venetian glass ware was exported to the Near East over a period of at least two centuries after 1500 and influenced the design and decoration of Persian glass in the period of Shah Abbas (1587–1628). According to the records of English travellers, Italian workmen were employed at the glass houses of Shiraz. A faint reflection of the *façon de Venise* may even be found in the glass ware of Mogul India, in the 17th and 18th centuries, which was probably made by Persian craftsmen from Shiraz. Thus the Venetians could almost literally claim to have captured a world market 'from China to Peru'.

Nevertheless, indigenous styles and traditions had only lain dormant. In Spain they were all that was left until the new factories were founded in the 18th century. In France, the discovery of plate glass casting robbed Venice of one of its most profitable markets. In England, after the invention of lead glass by Ravenscroft, Venetian imports fell almost to nothing in a matter of twenty years, and in Holland, where Venetian workmen were still employed in the early 17th century, there was a slow drift away from

A group of *façon de Venise* pouring vessels,
two *porros* and a *cantir*.
Barcelona, 17th century.
6¼, 11 and 8 in. high.

Richard Dennis

[5] His account bears quotation, showing how
primitive was the manufacture of *barilla*. ' I
am now come to Alicante for I am to send
hence a commodity called *barilla* to Sir
Robert Mansell for making of crystal glass
. . . this *barilla* is a strange kind of vegetable
. . . it grows thus, it is a round thick earthy
shrub that bears berries like barbaries
betwixt blue and green; it lies close to the
ground and when it is ripe they dig it up
by the roots and put it together in cocks
where they leave it to dry many days like
hay; then they make a pit of a fathom deep
in the earth and with an instrument like
one of prongs, they take the tufts and put
fire to them and when the flame comes to
the berries, they melt and dissolve into an
azure liquor and fall down into the pit till
it be full; then they dam it up and some
days after they open it and find this *barilla*
juice, turned to a blue stone, so hard that
it is scarce mallable; it is sold at 100 crowns
a tun . . .'. (Quoted in Frothingham, op.
cit., p. 12.)

the lightness of *façon de Venise*. In 1680 Liège was making 'flint glass à
l'anglais' and the search for a new metal led Dutch glass blowers to follow
German and English styles. But the decisive breakaway came with the
impact of the new crystal of Bohemia and Silesia. Some indication of
the force behind national competitiveness, and the difficulty of breaking
away from the Venetian glass houses, may be gauged from the visit by
an Englishman, James Howell, to Alicante in search of fine quality Spanish
barilla in 1621.[5] The need was inspired by the poor and bubbly nature of
the glass metal, which was all that could be created in England before
Ravenscroft. Similar difficulties were experienced in Germany and Holland,
where a great deal of 17th century work was subject to crizzelling or glass
sickness—a phenomenon in which the surface of the vessel first showed a
network of fine cracks, then exuded a sour smell and finally, if the blend
of the materials was very poor, decomposed completely.

However, after a period of perhaps fifty years of experimentation, the
deficiency in the ingredients was cured, in England by the addition of
lead oxide and in Germany by the substitution of potash for soda and the
addition of lime or chalk. Europe was suddenly presented with a new
form of the material, glass, itself—heavy, lambent and clear in a way which
had never been achieved by the Venetian *cristallo*. The universal fashion
for deeply cut and engraved glass thus set by Bohemia, which swept Europe
in the 18th century, at once put the Venetians on the defensive, for the thin
cristallo could not, of its nature, compete. In spite of the privilege given to
Briati by the Republic in 1736, and the attempts to try and emulate the
German composition, Venice never recaptured the primacy which she
had so long maintained.

German Glass to the end of the 18th Century

Three main classifications of German glass may be noted during the period ending in the last quarter of the 18th century. Vernacular green glass, whose most potent expression was the *Römer*, lasted throughout the *façon de Venise* period and survived far beyond and in revived forms up to the present day. Enormous quantities of green glass were made all over Germany and Austria, and it is impossible to assign a region to such examples, just as, after the 17th century, it is hard to date any particular example within a matter of fifty years. Repetitiveness did not destroy the vigour of the style, but the *Römer* did not recapture the massive dignity of the best early specimens.

The *Stangenglas,* of clear metal, enamelled in a light palette of colours, had developed into a significant form before the Venetian period, during which enamelled glass was regarded as a somewhat inferior branch of the art. The *façon de Venise* was then replaced by the deep cut, fine glass ware of Bohemia and Silesia, and enamelled glass never had the chance to rise to the first position. Nevertheless, its manufacture was widespread and as a truly national form of domestic art it is considered at some length below.

The demand for finest glass ware was filled by the clear engraved glass which is, of course, of small quantity in relation to the other two categories. For nearly a century, coloured glass was little represented in this bracket except for the ruby glass of Potsdam, opaque white glass and the elaborate varieties of decoration such as *Schwarzlot* and *Zwischengoldglas* described later.

Above
A decanter with enamelled and *latticino* decoration.
Saxony, 1649.

Corning Museum

Right
Passglass, dated 1719, painted in enamels, with a young girl, a stag, a hare and a wild boar, and an inscription on the reverse. (See page 44.)
German.
10 in. high.

Sotheby & Co.

Below
Halloren Humpen, enamelled and dated 1679.
Hall, Tyrol.

Corning Museum

Stangenglas, enamelled and dated 1678.
Germany.

An enamelled beaker.
German, late 17th century.
6½ in. high.

Leslie Scott

Something will be said of regional variations in enamelled glass but it should be remembered that in the 17th and 18th centuries German glass houses covered a very wide area which might be better described as central European. Manufacture had moved away from the Rhine in the Middle Ages and now centred on a number of regions, mostly mountainous and all well wooded: in the west, Hesse, stretching from Laubach to the Würzburg, including Spessart (where a famous ordinance regulating the glass trade was promulgated as early as 1406); further south to Würtemburg; in the north, Brandenburg (including Potsdam and Berlin) and Brunswick; in the centre, Thuringia, based on the forests of Kaufungerwald and the Reinhardswald, stretching south to join Franconia and Nuremberg. Then in the east, along the frontier of what was later to become Czechoslovakia, lay the mountains and forests: the Bayerischerwald and Böhmerwald separating Bavaria from Bohemia; the Fichtelgebirge between Franconia and Bohemia and the Erzegebirge and Riesengebirge along the frontier with Saxony and Silesia.

An enamelled decanter.
South German, late 17th century style.
8 in. high.

Leslie Scott

Silver-mounted Kunckel ruby glass teapot,
marked 'C.F.'.
Potsdam, *c.* 1700.
4½ in. high.

Sotheby & Co.

In the mid-16th century, not long after the evolution of the tall cylindrical *Stangenglas*, German glass makers began to decorate the clear surface with enamel painting. German enamelling cannot, however, be described as an art in the sense of the best Venetian or Catalan painting, because of its crude and repetitive nature. The painters themselves were craftsmen rather than artists and they not only worked on very large numbers of glasses but took their models for even the most elaborate designs from contemporary woodcuts and engravings. The itinerant habits of the skilled workmen make it difficult to attribute glasses, except by dates and coats of arms, and in contrast to the artists of the 18th century no particular names are known.

Good enamelled *Stangen* are not rare, but scarce; yet they were made in enormous quantities and presumably also broken on a grand scale. A glass maker at Cassel, for example, in 1657, undertook to make a thousand large beakers a year, in return for a concesssion from the Land Graf; while 20,000 glasses were ordered from Bohemia for the coronation of Christian IV of Denmark in 1596. The Laubach factory turned out 8,000 glasses *a week* in 1683. (The largest production was of course green glass and window glass. Hall in Tyrol was producing 3½ million panes of glass a year in the 1560s.)

Enamelling is found on beakers and other vessels, but the greatest part is on *Stangen*, or *Humpen* as they became known in the 17th century. A huge glass, often holding as much as half a gallon, is called *Wilkomm* from the verses which were painted on the side as a welcome to guests. The inscription of these usually begins 'Der Wilkomm bin ich gennandt . . .' (My name is Welcome . . .) and the, presumably, fortunate guest had to empty the whole glass himself. The enamel designs on *Humpen* are of great variety and the classification given to them follows that adopted by Dr Alex von Saldern in his monograph on the magnificent collection of German enamel glass in the Corning Museum of Glass, New York.

Façon de Venise

Most early glasses bearing German coats of arms were, as mentioned above, probably made to order in Venice; and the traditional attribution of 'Nuremberg glass' to the famous Augustin Herschvogel cannot be substantiated. However, by the mid-16th century armorial beakers and *Stangen* appeared, which can be attributed to southern Germany; most of these followed the Venetian tradition, with bands of enamel, dots and gilding, and scroll work around the main design. The existence of a skilled technique at Hall is an indication that Venice had no monopoly of enamel work. The tall *Stangen* are of thin clear metal, a fashion which changed about 1570 towards the heavier *Humpen*, characteristic of Bohemia. Enamelled *façon de Venise* glasses had virtually died out by 1600. Thereafter, the range of enamel ware widened considerably and the classes of the subject may be described separately.

Reichsadler Glasses

Perhaps the best known of all subjects is the double-headed eagle of the Holy Roman Empire, bearing a crucifix or an imperial orb on its breast. The wings are usually covered with 56 shields in rows and vertical groups of four. At the top are those of the Seven Electors of the Apostolic See; below are arranged the representatives of each profession and category within the Empire, an idealised theme which bore little relation to the tangled political structure of the Hapsburg domain. The earliest glasses are those with the crucifix, which date from the 1570s. Orb glasses start a decade later, but continue even to the mid-18th century. Like other subjects in enamels, the *Reichsadler* design is based on pictorial and literary sources dating from much earlier: the system was first described in 1460 and appears in a number of late 15th century woodcuts.

Kurfürster Humpen

Closely related to the eagle theme is that of the Emperor accompanied by the Seven Electors, either enthroned, with the Electors standing beside him, or all mounted on horseback in two horizontal rows. These glasses appear to have been as popular as the *Reichsadler* and like them show a large number of minor variations on the basic theme. The seated type date from 1591 to about 1650; the equestrian portraits are more numerous and range mainly from 1600 to 1670. Another variant of these two designs shows the portrait of the Emperor alone or with the arms of merchant guilds.

Portraits

An unusual category, possibly because of the crude and stylised nature of the work, even on the imperial *Humpen*. Some 17th century glasses show the monarchs of Saxony and Sweden and the Elector of Brandenburg.

Historical Glasses

Two series occur; the first made in Franconia commemorating the Treaty of Westphalia, which ended the Thirty Years' War—a matter, no doubt, of considerable rejoicing to that battle-scarred country. These show the Emperor standing in between the principal combatants, the King of France and the Queen of Norway, and the inscriptions praise peace and pray for a better future. The second type is represented on a single beaker (at Corning Museum) which shows the reformers, Luther and Melancthon, and two Saxon dukes, and commemorates the Reformation.

Biblical Glasses

These form a large category and range widely, from representations of the Twelve Apostles or the Four Evangelists, to the Adoration of the Kings and the Cruxifixion. Old Testament subjects include Daniel and the lion, Lot, the sacrifice of Isaac, and Jacob's ladder.

Allegorical, Erotic and Animalistic Glasses

Some *Humpen* show subjects from classical mythology, usually representing revels of Bacchus. Allegorical glasses are numerous: the Ages of Man, the Four Seasons, the Professions, the Virtues, variations of the theme of Memento Mori and the Dance of Death. Others follow an engraving of 1611 in satirical praise of idleness. A distinct group, called *Fichtelgebirge* glasses, from Franconia, show a symbolic view of a mountain, thickly wooded and full of game, with the high Ochsenkopf peak surmounted by a castle on the obverse. Many variations exist, all indicating the great forest and mineral wealth of the region. Painting and motifs more or less obscene, appear on many *Humpen*, the most popular of which shows a naked woman with a fox running between her legs. Foxes and geese and other animals appear also on a whole category of glasses, illustrating fables and peasant proverbs.

Hunting Scenes

Again two main types occur—on Bohemian glasses of the early 17th century which show hounds chasing stags or hares, and in a wide-spread series of *Humpen*, much more elaborate views of horsemen, followers hounds, in a boar hunt derived from 16th century woodcuts. Shooting contests and other forms of sport appear and there is a series of hunting enamels on *Römers*, probably from Hesse.

Costume and Genre Glasses

The majority of these show equestrian subjects or individuals in rich or strange costume. Some *Humpen* have lively paintings of drinkers, card players, musicians and dancers, or specific portraits of events.

Armorial, Guild and Family Glasses

These form by far the largest class of enamelled *Humpen* and extend to beakers, goblets, mugs and dishes. In Saxony there is a generic group called *Hofkellerei*. The most elaborate, as might be expected, are those which bear the arms of princely or noble families but the work is so wide-ranging as to be difficult to subdivide. Some examples bear twin shields to commemorate marriages and others the emblems of merchants, guilds, towns and corporations, or portraits of various trades and their activities, again usually taken from contemporary woodcuts.[6] Symbols of friendship and love occur—one inscription reads 'Ein hertze mus seyn auffrichtig, treu, standhafft' (a heart must be upright, true and constant)—and whole family groups are painted in procession, men on one side, women on the other.

[6] A well-known *humpen* dated 1680, in the Prague Museum, shows a view of the glass works at Zeilberg in Bohemia.

Pass Glasses

Stangen with applied horizontal rings of glass, or divisions painted in enamel, form a class by themselves. Enamel pass glasses were most popular from the mid-17th century to the early 18th. It became a matter of skill for each guest to drink exactly down to the allotted line and failure meant that he had to continue to the next. Pass glasses were decorated with a great variety of emblems, animals, figures and mottoes, ranging from pious exortation to the frankly pornographic. The glass illustrated (on page 39) bears the motto

Züchtig wie ein Jungfreulein	Chaste as a young virgin
Begierig wie ein Hirschlein	Desirous as a stag
Lustig wie ein Häslein	Merry as a hare
Besoffen wie ein altes Schwein	Drunk as an old pig

A blue glass tankard with a row of applied
prunts.
Bohemian, 17th century.
4½ in. high.

Sotheby & Co.

Other types of enamelled glass occur which do not fit these categories.
Some 17th century Bohemian coloured glass was painted, while others
bear simply floral and geometric patterns, or plain inscriptions. Painting
on *Milchglas* is described in the next section. By the early 18th century,
however, the quality of German enamelling was inclining to peasant-
types of glasses. Apparently made in Bohemia, Austria and Thuringia
for export abroad or for sale in country markets, this charming but crude
type of work flooded Europe with vessels of stereotyped decoration,
clumsily and rapidly executed. Small bottles, tumblers and flasks were
covered with floral motifs, or figurative subjects, animals and birds, like
doves perched on hearts, or foxes and geese, illustrating proverbs, in garish
reds, blues and yellows. As a form of folk art, 18th century German
enamelling deserves study, but at best, painters produced nothing but
imitation of what had gone before. Very similar glass painting was evi-
dently done in other parts of Germany, Switzerland and Holland. Un-
inspiring though the types are, however, the export trade laid the economic
foundation for the astonishing developments of Bohemian glass in the
early 19th century.

Attribution of the enamelled glasses to regions in Germany is a difficult
exercise. Apart from those of *Fichtelgebirge*, however, two notable classes
come from Saxony. *Hofkellerei Humpen*, made for the court, bear the Saxon
armorial shield and also the Polish arms after 1697, when the Elector,
Augustus the Strong, became King of Poland. Painting occurs in some cases
on *latticino* glasses. The second category of Saxon origin is the *Hallorenglas*,
made for members of the Guild of Saltmakers of Halle. They depict stylised
views of the town and members of the Guild at processions and festivals.

A blue glass flask with small protrusions on the surface and pewter mount. South German (*Alpenländisch*), 17th century. 6½ in. high.

Sotheby & Co.

Nearly all varieties of German enamelled glass were revived in the later 19th century, a conscious form of reproduction not unconnected with the search for a historic German identity which was intensified at the time of the unification of Germany under Bismark and the Prussian monarchy. Nothing could better symbolise the non-Latin, Teutonic past than the massive *Humpen* with its vivid national tradition of enamel decoration; and great numbers of skilful copies were made, some of which still cause confusion to collectors and specialists today. The firm of C. W. Fleischmann of Munich even issued a trade catalogue of enamelled glass reproductions about 1890. Copyists in Bavaria and Bohemia followed the old designs, especially the *Reichsadler* and *Kurfürster* paintings, but it should also be remembered that the production of peasant-type enamelled glass ran on to the end of the 19th century and does not represent a deliberate revival.

A polychrome enamelled covered goblet
in 17th century style, made by Lobmeyr
of Vienna.
Late 19th century.
12 in. high.

Richard Dennis

A covered goblet with colour-twist stem and applied cabuchons.
Bohemia, *c.* 1730.
9 in. high.

Richard Dennis

Other German Coloured and Painted Glass
The new metal, like rock crystal, which was developed in Germany about 1680, was made with potash instead of soda and with the addition of chalk. It was hard and brilliant, quite distinct from the deeper colour and soft lustre of English lead glass, and was a perfect substance for the relief cutting and engraving which had traditionally been used on rock crystal. The great age of Bohemian and Silesian glass followed and the technique spread outwards to Potsdam and Nuremberg. Since the work

A *Schwarzlot* beaker, dated 1667, on three bun feet, decorated with two man clasping hands and the motto: *Mein Hertz gib ich den Freund.*
Nuremberg, probably by a pupil of Johann Schaper.
4½ in. high.

Sotheby & Co.

was largely on clear glass, it may very briefly be summarised here.

Engraving with the wheel had been developed at Prague by Caspar Lehmann and his pupil George Schwanhardt at Nuremberg. By the late 17th century, a distinguished school of engravers was working at the latter city, and some of their pieces were of green glass, not unlike the earlier Hall goblets which had been engraved with diamond point. A certain amount of ruby glass was also decorated by Johann Heel, with birds and bunches of fruit in the style of contemporary painting on faience. But most of the engraving done in Germany in the period 1685–1775 was the work of unknown masters in Bohemia and Silesia. Here were carved the finest *Hochschnitt*, or deep relief vessels, with heavily knopped baroque stems, associated with the names of Winter and Spiller. The Bohemian art declined somewhat in the mid-18th century and its place was taken by Silesian work. Elsewhere, in Hesse, worked the great artist Franz Gondelach, and in Thuringia, members of the Sang family; while in Saxony, new factories were set up by E. W. von Tschirnhausen, collaborator with Böttger in the discovery of Meissen porcelain. At these factories stone ware was also cut and engraved like glass.

In one area, the manufacture led to a new form of coloured glass. A factory was founded at Potsdam in 1679 under the direction of Johann Kunckel, a chemist who had studied the classical work of Antonio Neri and written his own *Ars Vitraria Experimentalis*. Early Potsdam work, like much English glass, was subject to crizzelling, but was perfected in the 1680s. Some of the clear glass, in rather heavy forms, was engraved by Spiller and Gondelach. Gilding became quite common and in the early 18th century a whole group of engravers worked at Berlin. During

A beaker made in the *Zwischengoldglas* tradition, with amber and etched decoration.
Germany or Austria, *c.* 1830.
$3\frac{3}{4}$ in. high.

Howard Phillips

Kunckel's time, about 1679, ruby glass was first made by the addition of gold chloride. 'Kunckel glass' as it is sometimes called, has a marvellously rich quality and was greatly prized in the 18th century when its manufacture spread from Potsdam south to Nuremberg and Augsburg. Silver mounts added to the quality of mugs and bottles or the tea pot illustrated here. Kunckel also manufactured a deep blue glass, an emerald green, and an agate like the *vetro calcedonio* of Venice. A fine blue goblet with the engraved monogram of the Queen of Prussia is in the British Museum.

Kunckel experimented without great success on the making of a plain white glass which he called *porzellein-glas*. This was later manufactured in larger quantities in the 18th century in Saxony and at Basdorf in Prussia. *Milchglas* thus became virtually an international style, repeated at Bristol and La Granja in Spain, as well as Venice. The decoration is almost always similar to that of contemporary porcelain: flowers, rustic scenes, and subjects in the style of the *Hausmaler* (freelance artists working on factory porcelain in their own houses) of Meissen. Occasionally it is wheel engraved and gilt as well as enamelled. Some *Milchglas* work however, probably from Franconia, follows the style of earlier German enamelling on clear glass, with hunt or guild and trade representations. To what extent this opaque white glass was exported to Britain, France or Spain, or made in each of these countries, is not easy to determine.

Painters on glass existed in the 17th and 18th century who carried their work to an artistic standard far beyond that of the anonymous enamellers of *humpen*. A certain number of south German pieces were decorated in oil or lacquer colours, which, like the similar Venetian work,

A *Schwarzlot* beaker with caricature portrait after the French painter Callot. From the workshop of the Preissler family, *c.* 1680.

Private collection

A *Schwarzlot* beaker on three bun feet, with a hunting scene on a gold ground. Nuremberg, from the workshop of J. Schaper, *c.* 1650.

Private collection

A *Zwischengoldglas* beaker with polychrome body, decorated with an elaborate coat of arms and ruby glass base with floral medaliion.
Germany, early 18th century.
3½ in. high.

Sotheby & Co.

tended to wear rapidly away. Far more satisfactory was the style evolved in Nuremberg by the stained glass expert, Johann Schaper, after 1650. Schaper may be called the first of the *Hausmaler* and he worked mainly in black, heightened with a little red and gold in exquisitely fine brush-work—a technique known as *Schwarzlot*. Many of Schaper's designs on Nuremberg tumblers on three ball feet are signed. He was followed by the artists Johann Faber and Abraham Helmhack, and the *Schwarzlot* was copied in Bohemia and Silesia in the 18th century, particularly by members of the Preissler family. Landscapes and hunting scenes are typical of Nuremberg; later, the scenes were taken from peasant life or small *chinoiserie* subjects. *Schwarzlot* was a demanding skill and few examples are known after the mid-18th century; it was revived, however, with success by the glass works of Lobmeyr in the 19th century.

Other naturalistic flower and bird paintings on small bottles of about 1700 have been ascribed to Augsburg, although it is possible that they are of Venetian origin. The colours are light and include a strong purplish pink. All through the first half of the 18th century the *Hausmaler* tradition continued, as artists worked on porcelain as well as glass, which they bought from the factories. The latter bear motifs in the rococo style, views, hunting scenes, and figure subjects. The use of translucent stains, so much a 19th century Bohemian fashion, can already be found, usually in various shades of purple.

The last major German innovation of the 17th century looked back to the Roman technique of *fondi d'oro*. A glass vessel was ground down with great care for most of its height to fit a polygonal outer shell, leaving a small projecting shoulder at the top. Gold leaf was then stuck to the

A *Zwischengoldglas* goblet with gilding on
a ruby ground.
German, *c.* 1740.
6½ in. high.

Leslie Scott

inner vessel and engraved with a fine point. Silver leaf and coloured
enamel was sometimes added. At the base, similar work was executed on
a glass disc, usually backed with red or green lacquer. The base and the
outer case were then fitted over the inner shell. Called, appropriately
enough, *Zwischengoldglas*, the technique was extremely fine. Hunting scenes,
figures of saints (reminiscent perhaps of the Christian origins of the style)
and coats of arms predominate.

About 1775, the European fashion for glass engraving was replaced by
a vogue for facet-cut glass, set by English factories. The commercial
supremacy of Britain, which lasted until the first quarter of the 19th
century, had begun. Meanwhile, all over Europe, the neo-classical revival
replaced the baroque and rococo styles with a concentration on severity
and simplicity of form. In Germany, as in Spain and Italy, cylindrical
shapes and straight sided goblets ousted the elaborate stems and bowls
of Bohemia and Silesia. Silhouettes and portraits were the most decoration which the new fashion allowed and clear glass was used almost
universally. Colour indeed remained at a discount in Europe until the
remarkable transformation which followed the first quarter of the 19th
century.

Other 17th and 18th Century Glass

A *Milchglas* beaker decorated in enamels.
Bohemia, mid-18th century.

Sotheby & Co.

A bottle of onion shape (sometimes called a Heemskerk decanter) with hollow swan-necked handle.
Netherlands, c. 1685.
8¼ in. high.

Howard Phillips

The Netherlands
The long war of the Dutch against Spain finally ended in 1609, and the creation of the Dutch Republic split the Low Countries into Holland and Spanish Flanders, together with the Prince-Bishopric of Liège. Peace, and the great trading empire which the Dutch built up in the 17th century, inspired the foundation of new glass houses: at Middleburg, The Hague, Rotterdam and Amsterdam. Under the general characteristic of *façon de Venise* which lasted until the 1680s, no clear distinction can be made

between them and those of Antwerp and Liège.

A strong tradition of coloured glass existed, as shown above, in the elaborate Netherlands wine glasses, some of which had bowls of green or blue; and in the bottles of onion shape which were extremely popular. Other vessels had applied handles of coloured glass. The bottles appear in shades of deep green, blue, brown and purple or amethyst; some are mounted with silver tops and they are beautifully proportioned. They offered fine surfaces for engraving in diamond point, a technique almost certainly brought by workmen from Hall in Tyrol, and the most famous engraver has given the generic name of Heemskerk to the whole series. Willem van Heemskerk (1613–1692) was a cloth merchant and amateur artist who engraved mottoes, biblical verses and inscriptions in a stylish and flowing calligraphy. In many cases he added his signature, age and the date.

German influence pervaded Holland in the 17th century, not least because the fragile Republic had to lean on more powerful neighbours in war, first against Spain and then the France of Louis XIV. *Römers* and beakers akin to *Humpen*, and pass glasses in green glass and clear, were made in the Netherlands and are shown in numerous Dutch still-life paintings. The originator of calligraphic work, as far as is known, was Anna Roemers Visscher (1583–1651) who worked largely on green *Römers*, and engraved flowers, fruit and insects, as well as inscriptions, with a skill which even Heemskerk did not surpass. Her signed and dated pieces are of the greatest rarity.

Many unknown artists worked in diamond point on clear and coloured glass down to the 18th century, when the technique was replaced by that of wheel engraving. Late 17th century examples tend to show elaborate figure subjects or flowers, vine sprays, birds and foliage. By then, however, the glass makers had broken away from the *façon de Venise*. The search for a better metal than the Venetian *cristallo* was unsuccessful and at the end of the 18th century the whole Netherlands industry turned towards England. Liège made 'flint glass à l'anglais' and English workmen are recorded at Haarlem in the 1680s. Dutch glass of this period also follows English forms and like that of Germany as well, is usually badly crizzelled.

A pair of metal mounted blue glass bowls. Probably North Germany, late 17th century.
4½ in. high.

Sotheby & Co.

A gold painted plate with a genre scene. Probably Liège or France, 18th century.
Corning Museum

A blue glass decanter, facet cut and gilded with swags of flowers.
France, late 18th century.
11½ in. high.

Sotheby & Co.

In the period of William III and the Hanoverian successors of Queen Anne, Holland was closely linked with England, and the glass making of the Netherlands fell almost wholly under foreign domination. Especially after the Treaty of Utrecht in 1713, imports flooded in from Germany and England and by 1770 only the glass house of s'Hertogenbosch still flourished. The rest had turned to plain window glass, mirrors and wine bottles. Even Liège and the factory at Namur, founded in 1743, followed English styles, in a much inferior manner. Coloured glass almost ceased

A beaker decorated with the arms of Castile-Leèn, and the motto: *Viva el Rey de Espania.*
Spain, or bohemia, for export, mid-18th century.
$3\frac{1}{2}$ in. high.

Sotheby & Co.

to be made, except for the common green, although a number of imitations of English colour twist wine glasses were made, of blue or red threads of somewhat poor quality.

On Netherlands glasses, however, and imported lead glasses, chiefly from Newcastle, Dutch engravers created a tradition of wheel engraving and stippling which surpassed anything that England could produce. Since only clear glass was concerned, the work need not concern us here, except to mention the well known names of Jacob Sang, a wheel engraver who was related to the Sangs of Thuringia, and of the superb stipple engraver, Frans Greenwood. Stippling lasted until the middle of the 18th century, when its best exponent was David Wolff; it was revived some fifty years later by the Melort family.

For a hundred years or more after 1750, the Netherlands also produced a large quantity of clear glass ware decorated in enamels, almost identical with the Bohemian export industry. Small bottles, tumblers, beakers and glasses, and square moulded decanters with rounded shoulders are typical. They are painted in reds, yellows, blues, with a little green, and splashes of white. Some of them are gilt and though crude and repetitive, they all have a certain liveliness. The fact that they show figures and animals rather than just the stylised flowers of the Bohemian ware suggests that this is a form of folk art, worth collecting in the same way as the contemporary products of Nailsea and Stourbridge in England. Made to be sold at country fairs and exported to America, they probably existed in enormous numbers. They are difficult to date accurately and, as mentioned below, similar but rather more elegant things were also produced in Spain.

A tankard with cover, with gilt engraving
of fruiting vine, floral sprays and grasses.
La Granja de San Idelfonso, *c.* 1785.
11 in. high.

Howard Phillips

France

The only glass factory to survive strongly in France from the *façon de
Venise* period was at Nevers, where the Italian style lasted well into the
18th century. It is by no means clear where the glass ware for the Court
was produced, nor whether imports from Germany replaced what had
been a substantial French glass manufacture in the 17th century. Even
Nevers was famous chiefly for its glass toys—an obscure form which the
Prestereau family raised to high artistic standards in the early 17th century.

Animals and human figures were made of coloured glass by melting the end of a rod or tube, and manipulating or blowing the metal. Louis XIII, as a child, is supposed to have played with glass toys from Nevers. The most elaborate 18th century confections copied fine porcelain: groups of figures represented subjects such as the Four Seasons, the Commedia delle Arte, or the Crucifixion. Similar work was done at Rouen, Marseilles and Paris (all centres of porcelain or faience manufacture) and in the capital, Jacques Raux, a master of the fashion, advertised 'all sorts of grotesque figures for the decoration of cabinets and chimney pieces'.[7] But glass toys were not restricted to France and surviving examples, which are few, may also stem from Venice, Germany or Spain.

As Honey points out, the rest of 17th and 18th century French glass was almost wholly unexceptional and consisted of Netherlandish styles imposed on the vernacular tradition of *verre de fougère*. Indeed, as France lacked coal, all glass was still made in the ancient way. Nevers, Rouen and Orleans probably had a long continuity of manufacture, but except for a few coloured vessels, similar to English work, their output cannot

[7]Quoted in Honey, op. cit., p. 138.

A *Milchglas* tankard.
La Granja, *c.* 1770.
7 in. high.

Leslie Scott

be identified.

The invention of plate glass casting by Bernard Perrot of Orleans in 1680 established an entirely new French glass industry. The demands of the Court for mirror glass of all sizes and styles for the great rooms of chateaux and palaces, or boudoirs and cabinets, and for coach plate glass, attracted a flood of imports from Venice, which at the time of Colbert, were held to be a grave loss to the French Exchequer. In 1665 Colbert set up the 'manufacture royale des glaces de mirroir' in Paris, where

A facet-cut and gilt decanter.
La Granja, *c.* 1790.
11 in high.

Leslie Scott

Venetians were employed. After several years of experiment and with the use of Perrot's patent, the earliest royal factories were amalgamated at St Gobain in Picardy, under the title of the Royal Manufacture.

Normally, mirror glass would be outside the scope of this book, but in France the tradition of fine glass making under royal and aristocratic patronage lasted through the 18th century until the foundation of a number of new glass centres, which became famous in the 19th century for work of great elegance and subtlety. Otherwise, no great advance marked the mid-18th century when the acme of artistic achievement lay in the porcelain houses of Sèvres and Vincennes, and glass continued to be imported from abroad. Then, in 1760, the Academie des Sciences offered a prize for the best report and diagnosis of the failure of the French glass industry to compete. Whether the cures suggested were correct, or whether the next decade provided glass workers with a native style suited to their particular talents, the result was the foundation of the Baccarat factory near Lunéville, in 1765, and the Cristallerie de Saint Louis in Lorraine, in 1767. Others followed in the 1780s, and in 1800 the Chevalier d'Artigues opened a glass house at Voneche for the manufacture of clear glass, which was later transferred to Baccarat. By the end of the 18th century the name of Clichy was also established. All these made clear crystal very similar to the English style and presumably they reaped considerable commercial advantage during the Napoleonic wars, when English imports were cut off. The importance of the period, from the point of view of coloured glass, however, lies in the fact that a tradition of fine glass making had been created virtually from nothing in a matter of fifty years.

A decanter and two matching tumblers, with mould-blown bases, enamelled with flowers.
La Granja, *c.* 1800.
Decanter 10 in. high, beakers 3¾ in. high.
Richard Dennis

Spain

After near bankruptcy in the mid-17th century, the Spanish glass industry revived only slowly. In Catalonia, a Venetian style was carried on, but in a popular and debased form, and even the products of Barcelona seemed to have been designed for the tavern or the toy shop, rather than the sophisticated market. Typical of the period are vessels of purely Spanish origin and purpose – the *cantir* and *porro* for pouring wine, the *almorratxa*, double flasks for oil and vinegar, and oil lamps. They show a fanciful use of trailed and pincered ornament, applied in blue and white glass, and *latticino* in broad bands and splashes. Valencia came into prominence as a source of domestic glass ware, of *porros*, bottles and jugs in deep green and other coloured glass. And, centuries after the rest of Europe, a demand for window glass became widespread.

In Andalusia, in the south, a generic style of glass ware existed from the 16th into the 19th century, which was almost ignored elsewhere. Spread across the provinces of Almeria, Granada and Seville (though not in Seville itself, where *façon de Venise* glass ware was made), were a number of ancient houses making coloured glass in many shades of green, brown, purple, sapphire, cobalt blue and yellow, all in a very bubbly material. The use of two colours, or of a coloured overlay, is also known. The style of this southern art is vigorous but archaic in the extreme; reminiscent of Syrian and Islamic ware, and, in the extravagantly looped and fretted handles, of 4th century Rome. Most of the objects had spouts for pouring and the glass ware seems to have been intended purely for domestic use, just as in Granada today a peasant-style of pottery survives, decorated with ancient *mudejar* patterns.

The indigenous tradition was eventually weakened by the influx of Bohemian ware and of German glass traders, seeking through Seville and Cadiz a way into the vast market of Spanish America. About 150 German shops existed in Spain in the 1760s, a fact which explains the great quantity of cheap enamelled bottles and glasses which are often regarded as of Spanish origin. The illusion is fostered by crude and often inaccurate reproductions of Spanish and Portuguese coats of arms, patriotic motifs, mottoes in Spanish and figures in 18th century dress. Square, mould-blown Bohemian bottles in blue glass and opaque white are common, and sets of bottles and glasses in travelling cases for toilet waters or liqueurs.

The Spanish industry, weakened by the 17th century recession, struggled with difficulty against this competition. The Nuevo Baztan factory near Madrid, established in 1720 by Juan de Goyeneche, failed after a few years, despite some royal help. Later in the century, Charles III of Spain extended patronage to the Dorado family, who made fine, tall vases and goblets at the Recuenco glass house in the remote mountains of Cuenca. Direct exercise of patronage seems to have been necessary, because fine glass making in Spain, deprived of the more prosperous markets of England and Germany, could not survive on its own as an economic industry. Thus the royal house of San Ildefonso at La Granja, the summer palace in the mountains near Madrid, relied almost entirely on royal patronage and only rarely paid its way.

Established in 1728 by Buenaventura Sit, a Catalan, La Granja made some of the finest mirror glass in Europe for most of the 18th century. As at Recuenco and Cadalso, the fashion was for clear crystal in emulation of English glass, and La Granja made notable chandeliers, similar to the best Irish examples. Manufacture branched, however, to a soda lime glass of a pale greenish yellow tint, greatly prized as crystal in Spain. It was wheel engraved, simply and well, in the Bohemian tradition, but, unlike the latter, fire gilt in an entirely distinct fashion. In the last quarter of the 18th century the La Granja production was sold commercially in Madrid. The gilding was fine and lasted much better than that of Bristol or Bohemia. It was used sometimes to accentuate the cutting, or painted straight onto the glass, as is the case with the series of vessels bearing motifs from the royal arms—castles, lions, pomegranates or the Bourbon fleur-

A tumbler commemorating the fall of the Venetian Republic.
Venice, dated 1797.
4½ in high.

Leslie Scott

de-lys. The shapes of decanters, jugs and glasses bear a strong resemblance to those of England, even when the rococo style of engraving gave way to the more formal and stylised fruit and flowers of the neo-classical period.

La Granja failed to oust the cheap Bohemian imports either in Spain or the New World, but it gave rise to some excellent coloured and opaque white vessels. Antonio Neri's work on coloured glass, with Kunckel's additions, was translated into Spanish in 1775; and a fine purple vase is illustrated here. Opaque white glass rivalled that of Saxony and was used in a form of barrel-shaped drinking glass, with blue, red and white looped threading, not unlike Nailsea work. Chalcedony, agate and other semi-precious stones were simulated in what, by the 1780s, was a skilled and sophisticated manufacture. About this time, enamel painting on clear, blue and *Milchglas* reached a standard much higher than that of the Bohemian ware. Naturalistic flowers in subtler colours which are blended and shaded, rather than crudely painted, appear on glasses, decanters, beer and cider mugs and glasses, all of shapes very similar to English examples. Pharmacy jars and tall covered jars with handles and gilt rims were popular, and mould blown decanters with fluted sides and moulded stoppers, usually in sets with wine glasses. Though most of the painting was competently done in the workshop, certain artists, like the German *Hausmaler*, worked at home on the porcelain of Buen Retiro (Madrid) and on the finer glass of La Granja.

A radical change occurred soon after 1800, when the style changed completely to heavy glass, deeply cut in the Irish style. The transition was not unconnected with Spanish dependence on England at the time of the Napoleonic wars, and although some of this crystal was gilded, the use of coloured glass declined. The metal could not compare with lead glass and in 1809 Joseph Bonaparte, newly crowned King of Spain, abandoned the royal patronage.

Without this protection, La Granja went out of business. It was revived in 1814 and had a brief period of distinction, producing mould blown glass, usually engraved with romantic landscapes, but it operated irregularly thereafter. A school of painting in oils was inspired by the artist, Vicente Lopez, in the 1820s, but despite a notable showing at the Exposicion Industriale in 1845, La Granja soon lost its independent existence.

An oval silhouette medallion in *verre églomisé*.
Schlesien, Warmbrunn; possibly by Johann Sigismund Menzel, *c.* 1800.

Howard Phillips

The Early 19th Century and the Growth of European Styles

A tumbler with portrait medallion by
J. J. Mildner.
Late 18th century.
5 in. high.

Leslie Scott

The greatest social, political, economic and intellectual ferment in Europe since the Renaissance occurred at the end of the 18th century and in the early 19th. In many ways, the changes can be traced in the period before the French Revolution but they were given a physical impetus by the Napoleonic wars, and the redrafting of the map of Europe which could not wholly be undone after 1815. At the same time, a profound economic transformation was beginning in France and Germany, parallel to the industrial revolution in England, and in the mid-19th century came the transport revolution, bringing railways to every part of Europe. An equally revolutionary change occurred in society, leading irrevocably to what the French historian, Charles Morazé, has called the triumph of the middle classes. Attitudes of mind had to come to terms with the speed of change itself, and with all the consequences of the transition from an aristocratic oligarchy to new forms of government and society.

Europe and America were expanding in wealth and demands and the markets created by the economically dominant middle class were reflected in changing taste. The domestic arts were affected no less than contemporary literature, painting and sculpture. Thus began what in Germany is called the age of Biedermeier—the equivalent of the English romantic era or the bourgeois France of Louis Philippe. On crucial occasions after 1815, political events altered the pattern: revolution broke out again in 1830 and in 1848. The latter, the 'revolution of the intellectuals', led briefly to new governments which seemed to fulfil, in political terms, the rise of bourgeois society; but it was followed by repression in Vienna, Paris and Berlin, which, to the articulate liberal world, seemed a reversion to military barbarism.

Without linking the fashions for fine and domestic glass ware too closely to such changes, there can be no doubt that in Europe, as in England, styles did follow the demands of the market. The characteristics of the early 19th century were a revulsion from the formal magnificence of the rococo and a concentration on the plainer forms of the neo-classical style. In quantity, by far the greatest part of European glass ware was made in Germany, where, within the romantic age, two periods can roughly be discerned: the Empire, from the 1790s to about 1820; and the Biedermeierzeit from the 1820s to the 1840s. The former is notable for the simplicity even severity, of forms of glasses and the superb decoration of a few gifted artists; the latter brought a coarser, heavier type of glass, with much greater variety of decoration, and it is usual to disparage it as a time of placid bourgeois taste, the forerunner of mid-19th century philistinism. Certainly, fashion dictated glasses with naturalistic designs and paintings of landscapes for a largely tourist market; but it is not necessary to go so far as the French art historian, Louis Reau, and say that German domestic art is only 'a bastard version of the Empire style adapted to the needs and requirements of the provincial petty bourgeoisie'.[8] The variety and excellence of the Bohemian and German factories can be gauged from the examples illustrated here. The decline is better dated after the 1848 Revolution, in the period of revivals, which was not unconnected with the political and social repression of Bismarck's Prussia and Hapsburg Austria.

Germany and the Empire Style
The most typical glasses of the neo-classical period are urn-shaped vases and fluted or facet-cut cylindrical tumblers, and later, the *Ranftbecher*, a trumpet-shaped tumbler with a wider, flute-cut or faceted base. At the end of the 18th century, these were still wheel engraved but the cameo encrustations of Desprez (see page 79) and Apsley Pellatt were widely copied early in the 19th. Silhouettes and engraved portraits were common and some objects were mounted in elaborate ormolu in the French style.

The major innovation was the invention of painting in transparent enamel colours, full of romantic feeling for landscape in its wilder aspects —ruined castles, mountains and gothic fantasies. A fascination for classical scenes reflected the imperial illusions of the Napoleonic rulers. At the end of the Empire period, painting was given a further impetus by the fashion for souvenirs. Tourist mementoes of an expensive and delicate kind, recalled memories of Rome, or the churches of Dresden, or the palaces of Charlottenburg and Wilhelmstahl.

A school of artists grew up, following the traditions set by Samuel Mohn (1762–1815), who settled in Dresden in 1809, and his son, Gottlöb Mohn (1789–1825), who worked chiefly in Vienna. The father was first a painter of silhouettes on china. He gravitated to glass, where he repeated the silhouette patterns but added a whole repertoire in the most delicate designs and colours which had probably ever been seen in Europe—views of cities, churches and mountains. Gottlöb Mohn worked chiefly on tumblers and carried his father's technique to more romantic lengths: ruined castles, pastoral landscapes and sentimental allegories predominate. Some show only flowers; others, like the view of St Helena in 1815, were made to commemorate great events. His followers worked in Dresden, Vienna and Berlin and probably in most of the best glass houses in Germany. Glasses by any of them are prized by collectors and are never cheap; signed pieces by the Mohns are of great value.

The technique of painting in such fine and transparent enamels was further developed in Vienna by Anton Kothgasser (1769–1851), a former pupil of Gottlöb Mohn. In contrast to the latter, most of Kothgasser's work is found on the later *Ranftbecher*, usually with gilt enrichments. Portraits, cathedrals, views of cities, palaces and landscapes, moonlit skies, illustrations of proverbs, and coy maidens in brilliant colours, show the height of romantic, sentimental Biedermeier taste. Several examples are stained with a background of deep yellow made from a compound of silver.

Bouquets of flowers, birds and urns are found on less expensive work. Similar glasses were painted by F. A. Siebel of Lichtenfels in Franconia, at the studio of Egermann in Blottendorf, and in various other houses in North Bohemia.

Of the Empire period, but different in technique, were the medallion portraits of J. J. Mildner (1763–1808) of Gutenbrunn in Austria. Broadly speaking, he used the *Zwischengoldglas* method, but only in the ovals or panels which held the silhouettes or coloured portraits. Again, he worked mainly on tumblers and beakers, many of opaque white glass. The portraits in themselves are excellent miniatures and are surrounded with borders of intricate gilding and translucent coloured enamel. Entwined initials and views are also known, and sometimes the portraits were inserted in the base of the vessel instead. The technique was used later in commercial production—particularly on broadly fluted salt cellars with stylised portraits on a stained coloured ground set into the base.

The Age of Biedermeier

Meanwhile, in Bohemia, the fashion for heavily cut clear glass ware died out and was replaced by the most remarkable vogue for colour ever to sweep across Europe. In addition to the greens, blues and ruby reds known before, new shades of yellow, green or topaz were developed with the use of uranium and antimony. The names of *Annagelb* and *Annagrün* were given to two shades of opalescent green by the manufacturer Joseph Riedel. *Chrysophase* was another. *Milchglas* was developed, particularly to make the famous Bohemian overlay in which a vessel of one colour was coated with opaque white, which was then cut away in facets, lozenges or panels to reveal the layer beneath. Two and three layers were used for the finer pieces and the panels were then painted or engraved. A third form of colour decoration was the use of staining in red, silver yellow, topaz and green. Finally, there was the category of new mixtures of glass —*Hyalith*, a dense black glass, admirably suited for gilding, and red glass like sealing wax, was made after 1820 at the glass houses of G. F. A. Longueval, Graf von Buquoy. Black glass was also made at Zechlin during the Empire and various shades of deep marbled glass were developed by Friedrich Egermann (1777–1864) at his factory at Blottendorf in Bohemia in the late 1820s. These he called *Lithyalin*: they range from brick reds streaked with green to dark blues and purples.

The variety of decorated glass produced from 1820–50 in Bohemia was vast and despite the number of pieces illustrated, nothing but a brief survey can be given here. The pioneer work of Gustav Pazaurek, *Gläser der Empire und Biedermeierzeit*, published forty years ago, remains the standard text.

Enamel Painting on Clear and Opaque Glass

Normally in this period, on overlay glasses, the painters followed the styles of Mohn and Kothgasser, filling the large panels with views, and adding gilt and coloured motifs on the white surface. On coloured glass and on the *hyalith* and dark Egermann glass they worked in gilding or relief enamel, imitating the Wedgwood factory in England. The painting varies greatly in standard according to the market—export production for Europe and America was generally repetitive and done in the workshop, but fine glass ware for the expensive taste was painted with great distinction. Some identifiable artists still followed the *Hausmaler* tradition and worked independently, or followed the tourist trade to the fashionable spas, such as Karlsbad, Marienbad or Teplitz.

Gilding and Silvering

In addition to fine gilding, some glasses were decorated with a layer of gold or silver in high relief, in arabesque or rococo patterns. Gilt pictures were done, particularly chinoiserie figures on Graf Buquoy vases and urns, and in varied styles in the 1830s on the innumerable objects made of *hyalith* and the *lithyalin* of Egermann.

Glass Pearl Work

Tiny beads of coloured glass, strung together to form floral patterns like Berlin woolwork, were stretched round the sides of the *Ranftbecher* or sometimes over the whole of a bottle or flask. Similar painstaking work appears on purses and other articles of domestic embroidery.

Venetian and Other Imitations

Latticino, *aventurine* glass and *millefiori* patterns were all copied during the

A beaker with a view of a country estate.
School of Kothgasser.
Vienna, *c.* 1835.
5½ in. high.

Richard Dennis

A beaker with a view of Tharaud, signed
S. Mohn fec. 1812.
Dresden.

Private collection

A *Milchglas* beaker with a portrait medallion in the style of Mildner.
c. 1820.

Leslie Scott

Right
A *hyalith* goblet, black glass elaborately gilt, with *Zwischengold* medallion of Justice.
Bohemia, *c.* 1830.
$7\frac{1}{8}$ in. high.

Sotheby & Co.

A *lithyalin* beaker by Egermann with alternate coloured panels, gilt flowers and insects and the inscription *Erinnerung* (Remembrance), and a *lithyalin* scent bottle and snuff-box with ormolu mounts.
Beaker $4\frac{1}{8}$ in. high, snuff-box $2\frac{1}{2}$ in. diameter.
Sotheby & Co.

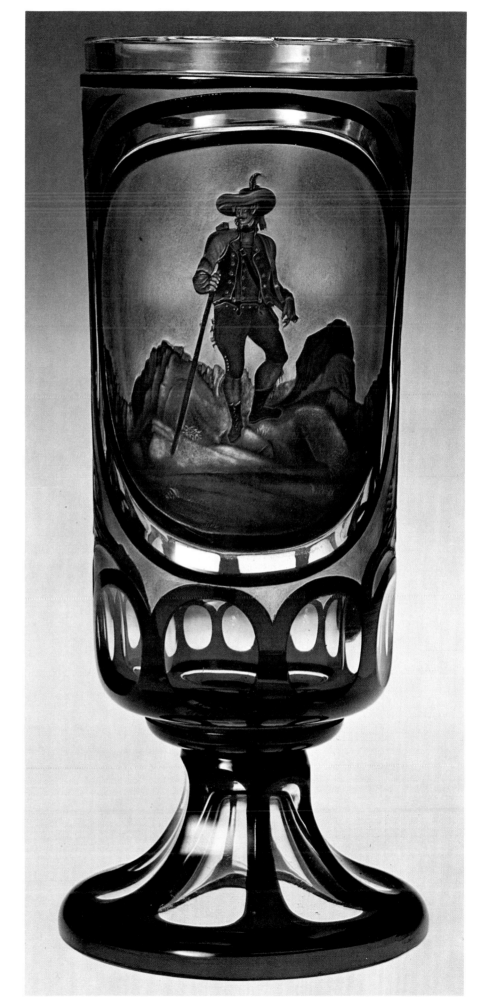

Above left
A rare *lithyalin* glass beaker signed *F. Egermann* in gilt and decorated with a full length figure in gilding.
A gilt *lithyalin* beaker with foliate motifs. Probably Haida.
5¼ and 5⅛ in. high.

Sotheby & Co.

Below left
Three *lithyalin* beakers by Friedrich Egermann of Blottendorf, one inscribed with the name *August Saatzer*.
4¼ in. high.

Sotheby & Co.

A red overlay goblet engraved with a figure of a mountaineer.
Bohemia, *c.* 1845.
8½ in. high.

Richard Dennis

Biedermeier period, as they were to a lesser extent in France. In a different category, the encrusted cameo work of Desprez was followed in Bohemia, in medallions, heavily cut beakers and flasks, with portraits of generals or royalty, down at least to the 1840s.

Engraved Glass

Engravers worked on clear, stained or overlay Bohemian glass in styles designed for what was, by the end of the 1840s, a considerable export trade. The great majority of pieces show a fairly stylised range of subjects, akin to the painted scenes—views of cities and public buildings, landscapes and portraits, cut through the staining or overlay to reveal the design in clear glass—but a whole genre of hunting and sporting scenes and pictures of animals and horses was developed in the 1840s. Some of the best articles equalled the former Bohemian standards. Dominic Bimann (1800–1857), an engraver of exquisite portraits and landscapes, worked in Prague, but like many of the painters, spent the fashionable season at Franzensbad, taking commissions and working on special orders. The names of Johann Pohl, August Böhm and the families of Pelikan of Meistersdorf, Simms of Gablonz, and Moser, are also famous. Scarcely less competent is the work of the anonymous artists in the factories at Karlsbad and at Neuwelt, Zwiesel, and the Isergebirge in Bohemia.

Engraving and other forms of decoration did not cease after 1850. Indeed the export of Bohemian glass was, in quantity, only just developing. Between 1876 and 1880, for example, $3 million worth of 'Bohemian glass cut, engraved, painted, coloured, printed, stained, silvered or gilded, plain mold and pressed' glass was imported into the United States. But

A flashed, engraved and damascened vase.
Bohemia, *c.* 1840.
8 in. high.

Richard Dennis

A goblet with views of spas.
Hungary, *c.* 1835.
7 in. high.

Private collection

the work which followed was undeniably repetitive, even from relatively new factories like that of J. & L. Lobmeyr, founded at Vienna in 1823. The best testimony to the age of Biedermeier can be found in the catalogues issued by various firms in the 1830s and '40s, when the enormous range of styles and the bewildering variety of subjects, including glass vases, inkstands, cruets and scent bottles, tumblers, flasks and door knobs, urns and ornaments, was all set out. It was a period of comfortable confidence, lacking inspiration except in the best examples, but showing in the domestic market a vivid imagination and even a touch of fantasy.

France

During the Empire and later, in the period of Louis Philippe, which corresponds to Biedermeier, the French glass industry developed several new techniques with an elegance and perfection of workmanship which entitles the houses of Baccarat, Clichy and Saint Louis to a high place in glass history. But the greater part of ordinary manufacture was devoted to cut or engraved, stained and overlay glass, in styles almost identical with those of Bohemia. Already, it may be said, there was an international market in glass, based on the requirements of Britain, Germany and the United States, the three nations who were becoming industrialised faster than the rest. Difficult as it is to distinguish overlay made in France from Bohemian, it is harder still to separate French examples of *latticino* work— of which a great amount was made, especially at Choisy-le-Roi, under the direction of Georges Bontemps, in the 1840s and '50s. But the cameos of Desprez, *millefiori* work, and opaline glass deserve special mention.

Cameo Encrustation

The Desprez family, working in Paris, evolved the technique of enclosing white cameos and medallions, akin to porcelain, in clear, heavily cut crystal. The development was apparently quite independent of that done by Apsley Pellatt of England. Like James Tassie, who began by making ceramic portraits, Desprez made cameos of porcelain or glass paste, and, early in the Empire period, started to set them in clear glass. A number of factories followed the example and by the 1840s they were being enclosed in paperweights at Baccarat. The *millefiori* paperweights which flowed from the factories of Saint Louis, Baccarat and Clichy, and the great number of patterns, ranging from simple flowers to the rarest swans and salamanders, cannot be discussed here, but they were undoubtedly the fashionable sensation of the 1840s all over Europe.

Opaline Glass

Coloured and white opaque glass, called *opaline* in France, came suddenly into fashion in the 1820s. As the *Journal des Dames et des Modes* of January 1824 noted: 'On a donné aux dames, en cadeau de Jour de l'An, beaucoup de cristaux colorés en blanc laiteux dit opale; en rose, dit hortensia; en bleu dit turquoise; et en verte, emeraud'.[9] (The ladies were given, as a New Year's gift, many coloured crystals in white opaque glass, called opal; in pink, called hortensia; in blue, called turquoise; and in green, called emerald.) Opaline glass had been known in Venice and Bohemia and was written of by Neri and Kunckel, but in France, where it was set in ormulu, or lavishly decorated like Sèvres porcelain, it became a sophisticated art form, far beyond the *Milchglas* of Bristol or La Granja.

Apart from a few examples made during the Empire and mounted in ormulu, opaline remained subsidiary to the taste for clear crystal, whose European market was assured by the prohibition of English imports during the Napoleonic wars. Thereafter, the French glass houses had to face the full competition of Bohemia and Britain, and for a matter of thirty years the three countries vied with each other in almost identical productions and at a whole series of international exhibitions.

Opaline glass was something apart, at which France excelled. The glass metal, whether of clear or opaque colour, resembled porcelain in every way, except for its translucent nature, which in white glass gave

[9] Quoted in Yolande Amic, *L'Opaline Français au 19th siecle* (Paris, 1953), p. 11.

off a deep orange fire. Indeed it may be called a divergence from the main stream of glass history, like the *hyalith* and *lithyalin*. Apart from white opaline, the period from 1820–30 was characterised by a soft palette of colours, not unlike 18th century porcelain—turquoise blue, rose pink, green and violet. After 1830, under the monarchy of Louis Philippe and following Bohemian influence, the colours became harder—*bleu céleste*, *bleu d'outremer*, *gris pigeon*, and the uranium greens and yellows.

The shapes followed porcelain manufacture closely; simple neo-classical forms under the Empire, then showing Chinese influences, and echoes of the polygonal designs of Bohemian glass in the period 1840–70. Turkish style followed—a fanciful recreation of the Orient with waving fronds on the bodies of vases, and vases 'de fantaisie' or, more simply, trinkets. Just as fine English cameo cutting was mechanised, so by 1870 opalines were made for a wide market, 'opaline de bazar' as their historian remarks.

Opaline glass, of course, provided a superb surface for painting and gilding, quite apart from the intrinsic beauty of the translucent material. While most early examples are plain, or mounted with ormolu handles and ormolu for the lids of boxes, stoppers, or the framework of chandeliers, gilding and silvering of exquisite delicacy was usual in the 1820s and '30s. Unfired colours were used for painting before 1835, and thereafter, fired metallic oxides. The work is too fine and rare for any standard to be defined, but most of it consisted of flowers, butterflies, insects and animals. Among the names of many artists, probably the best known is that of Jean-François Robert, whose workshop was responsible for a large number of the finest opaline pieces. Other forms of decoration included impressed patterns in the glass and the use of overlay and *pâte de verre*—the latter an innovation which was to be important in the origins of art nouveau in France, when the opalines had fallen into decadence.

Venice

In the early 19th century, Venetian glass making also revived, though it followed the fashion set by Germany. Wheel engraved cylindrical beakers bearing portraits and simple neo-classical scenes were made, and conscious revivals of antiquity took place. They gave rise to expensive murrhine bowls, beakers and tazzas, and *latticino* covered cups reminiscent of the 16th century, and, perhaps for export to England, large centre pieces in the form of fruit stands, with borders of variegated colours. As yet, however, there was no radical innovation in the form of glass. This was to follow elsewhere in the late 19th century, but the revival of the Renaissance style, by Antonio Salviati, who took pride of place at the International Exhibition in Paris in 1866, showed the beginnings of rethinking traditional modes, which was to be a formative influence in other areas of Europe.

A red stained goblet and cover engraved
with a portrait of the King of Poland.
Bohemia, *c*. 1840.
10 in. high.

Leslie Scott

The Later 19th Century

A time of stagnation followed the exuberance of the age of Biedermeier. For about thirty years, European glass seemed to lose its originality. Probably the chief reason was the way in which Bohemian and French factories had become tied to mechanical production for export, but it does seem that there was a distinct falling off in artistry and inventiveness. Vast quantities of overlay glasses, vases and lustres crossed the Channel or Atlantic to grace the cabinets of middle class families. It is not too much to say that Bohemia dominated the world, as Venice had in the 17th century, yet the result was not inspiring. A whole series of revivals followed, inspired partly by nationalist themes, such as the unification

Above
An amethyst overlay goblet and cover engraved with a portrait of the King of Poland.
Bohemia, *c.* 1840.
9½ in. high.

Leslie Scott

Overlay beakers with views of spas.
Bohemia, *c.* 1840.
5½, 7, and 4¼ in. high.

Richard Dennis

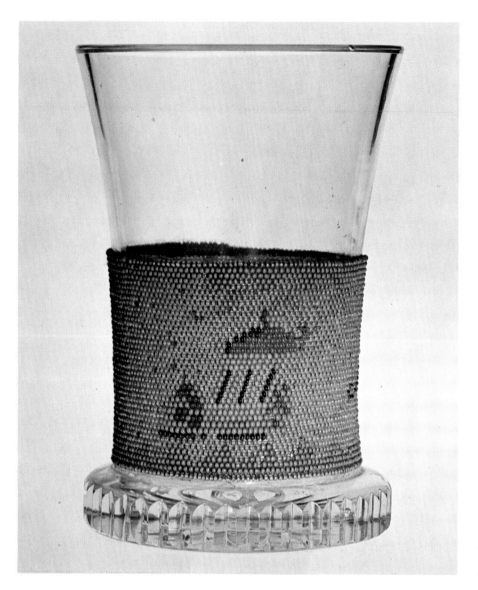

Above and *right*
Two beakers, one in red overlay, the other
of green opaline.
Bohemia, *c.* 1850.

Leslie Scott

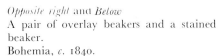

Opposite right and *Below*
A pair of overlay beakers and a stained
beaker.
Bohemia, *c.* 1840.

Leslie Scott

of Germany, and partly by the formation and publication of museum collections of antique glass ware. In Bohemia, as shown earlier, this gave rise to imitations of enamel painting in 16th and 17th century styles. The fine glass works of Lobmeyr in Vienna, for example, produced *Schwarzlot*, an example of which is illustrated. Similar archaism descended on France, but research into glass technology prepared the way for the very different style of art nouveau.

In Bohemia, where in the 1870s the industry was still remarkably primitive (only twelve out of 169 major furnaces burnt coal), the Austrian Government likewise stimulated schools of design and decoration, and the research that was undertaken emerged in a number of new forms of glass which were later taken up in England and the United States. By the 1880s, the world market was so competitive that the innovations which had been developed in the latter countries were also put into large scale production in Bohemia.

Pearl Satin Glass
In a very large number of shades, satin glass emanated from French and Bohemian factories up to 1896. Some examples bear marks identical with Sèvres porcelain and in general they were advertised widely in trade journals. The firm of Lazarus and Rosenfeld of New York, who distributed what they called 'Bohemian art glass ware' advertised lamps and vases in 'Rose de Bohème, Green de Bohème' and so on in the late 1880s, and the cheaper satin glass from the factories of Altrohlau and Steinschönau had a depressing effect on the manufacture of the better English and American equivalents.

Spun Glass

By the 1830s, it had become possible to make spun glass in fibres or filaments as fine as silk threads. The invention, which was widely used in the making of glass novelties, like the pyramids of birds from Stourbridge in England, is usually credited to D. Bonnel of Lille, who patented it for European countries in 1837. Cloth of glass fibres was made into dresses and church vestments, rivalling threads of gold or silver, and an extraordinary lifelike figure of a lion in spun glass was exhibited at Paris in 1855. Specially woven fibres and decorative birds ornamented with plumed tails were made down to the end of the 19th century.

Silvered Glass

In Europe this manufacture was mainly an extension of the patent taken out in England in 1843 for coating the interior surface of a hollow glass with a type of silver lustre. Like English and American products, mid-19th century European silvered glass was made in jugs, goblets and other domestic forms, and also as elaborate ornaments for Christmas trees.

A white overlay carafe and matching tumbler, cut with ovals decorated in gilding and enamels.
Bohemia, c. 1850.

Sotheby & Co.

Lava Glass

The French chemist, J. A. Chaptal, working for the Queen of Naples in the late 18th century, succeeded in making a form of marbled glass by mixing volcanic slag with the batch of ingredients. The effect was of velvety purple stone, and it was repeated in France in the early 19th century. Objects in lava glass, usually boxes, candle sticks and table ornaments, were also made in Bohemia, and in the 1880s the fashion was taken up in England under the name of slag glass.

Iridescent Glass

The surface decay obtained on Roman glass by long burial in damp earth was extremely attractive to the glass makers, who attempted to overlay their material with a finely ridged metallic film which would produce the same effect, by differential refraction. The firm of Lobmeyr exhibited iridescent glass in 1873 and commercial production followed at Neuwelt in Bohemia. In 1879, distributors of Bohemian glass in New York announced the arrival 'from Bohemia of the finest selection of iridescent

A pair of green and white overlay lustres. Bohemia, *c*. 1850.

Leslie Scott

glass and bronze glass ever assembled under one roof'.[10] In 1887 the same firm, Henrichs and Co., offered Bohemian 'nacre de perle' ware, and also iridescent glass from Salviati's factory in Venice. France also produced iridescent glass after 1857, when a method was patented by J. J. H. Brianchon.

Tortoise-shell Glass
An interesting, rather involved innovation, was patented by Francis Pohl in Silesia in 1880. The method was to insert fragments of brown glass into clear bubbles and then stain the whole vessel yellow. It was widely imitated elsewhere.

Developments of earlier techniques also took place in the later 19th century, usually designed to adapt a skilled and lengthy process to something like mass production. Cameo encrustation, for example, did not cease after the vogue for French paperweights in the 1840s; portraits were enclosed in clear, coloured and opaline glass in France and Bohemia down to the 1880s, when they seem to have fallen out of fashion.

Millefiori and Latticino Glass
Very detailed portraits, of passable likeness, were developed at Murano in the 1860s by Franchini and Moretti; the faces were made up of a large number of minute rods with several different skin tones to give realism. Commercial production of ordinary *millefiori* work, bowls, paperweights and trinkets, of course, continued throughout the 19th century. The same

An overlay goblet decorated in enamels with full length figures, and a similar overlay goblet.
Bohemia, *c.* 1840.
6 in. high.

Sotheby & Co.

[10] Quoted in A. C. Revi, *19th Century Glass* (London, 1959), p. 215.

Right
A beaker painted in a crude style with a steam train.
Bohemia, *c.* 1860.
4 in. high.

Richard Dennis

Above
A blue opaline inkwell, salt cellar and
two small jugs.
France, *c.* 1830.

Leslie Scott

is true of *latticino* work which in Bohemia, under the name of *Netzgläser*, was wrought in a ribbed, reticulated form on the inside and outside of glasses. The use of colour stripes, in between the white, in 19th century Venetian style, was imitated in France and Bohemia after the Salviati revival, especially at Neuwelt and Josephinenhütte.

The secret of aventurine or spangled glass was rediscovered as a commercial proposition in France in 1860, breaking a Venetian monopoly which had existed for centuries. Pink, green and bronze aventurine was often incorporated in larger vessels of clear or cut glass.

Cameo Glass

European artists attempted the lengthy and difficult technique of carving cameos on overlay glass. A number of fine pieces, with classical figures in white on deep blue ground, like those of Northwood of Stourbridge, were made in Venice. In France, cameo carving became a facet of art nouveau. The Bohemian factories, following the English habit of mechanical production, flooded the European and American market with imitations in very flat designs, made rapidly with the use of hydrofluoric acid. In the

A snuff-box with a sulphide portrait of Napoleon, from the sculpted portrait by Andrieu.
Paris, possibly from the workshop of Desprez, c. 1820.
3¼ in. diameter.

Richard Dennis

1890s 'Florentine art cameo' and 'lace de Bohème cameo', sold in quantity by Lazarus and Rosenfeld in New York, undermined completely the market for hand-made cameo glass and eventually destroyed the demand. In the same debased category is the so-called 'Mary Gregory' glass—coloured Bohemian ware with figures and children in 19th century dress, painted in white enamel. Mary Gregory was popularly supposed to have painted this type of glass at the Sandwich factory in the United States, but it was in fact chiefly imported from Europe.

A grey opaline urn.
France, *c.* 1810.
11 in. high.

Leslie Scott

Pâte de Verre
Coloured glass ground into powder and then mixed with a flux and refired, produces moulded vessels with a finely pitted, velvety surface. The technique, which was known in ancient Egypt, was revived in the 1880s by Henri Cros in France and it formed the basis for some of the work of the great artists of the art nouveau period.

Left
A pair of pedestal vases, with banded, urn-shaped bodies and with gilt decoration of flowers and foliage in festoons, ribbons, stars, tassels and floral sprigs.
France, *c.* 1800.
13½ in. high.

Howard Phillips

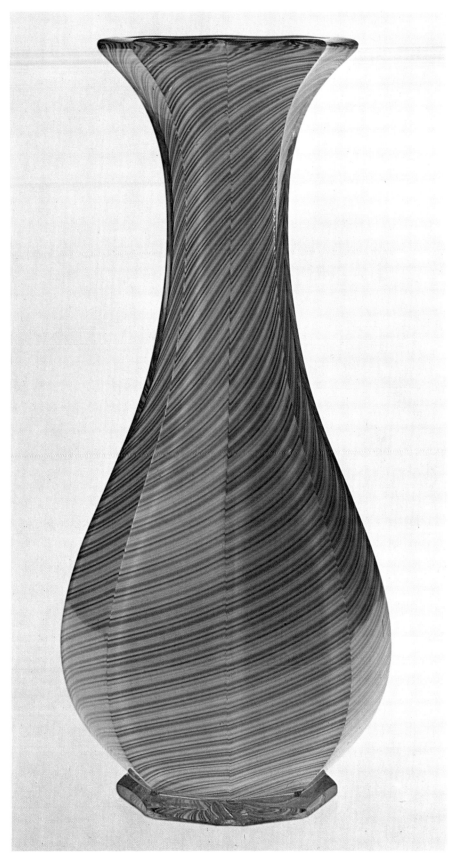

A Clichy *latticino* vase.
France, *c.* 1840.
6½ in. high.

Leslie Scott

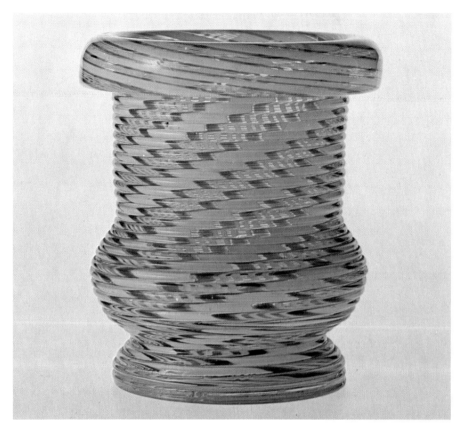

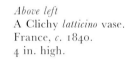

Above left
A Clichy *latticino* vase.
France, *c.* 1840.
4 in. high.

Leslie Scott

Above
A blue covered urn.
Norway, *c.* 1810.

Corning Museum

Opposite page
Above right
A black glass and gilt tea service.
Bohemia, from the factory of Graf Bucquoy,
c. 1840.

Leslie Scott

Right
A set of blue moulded tea caddies.
Russia, *c.* 1860.

Leslie Scott

Left
A *Milchglas* beaker decorated with Hungarian patriotic emblems, probably made to commemorate the 1848 Revolution.
Hungary.
$4\frac{3}{4}$ in. high.

Leslie Scott

Art Nouveau

A Gallé vaseline glass bowl, painted and enamelled with seaweed and shells.
c. 1889
4 in. high.

Richard Dennis

Opposite page
A Gallé vase in the form of a flower, enamelled with fruiting branches and insects.
c. 1884.
6½ in. high.

Richard Dennis

Over pages
Left
A Gallé vase carved with poppies. c. 1895.
17½ in. high.

Right
A Gallé *vase de tristesse*, carved with shell and seaweed decoration. c. 1895.
11½ in. high.

Richard Dennis

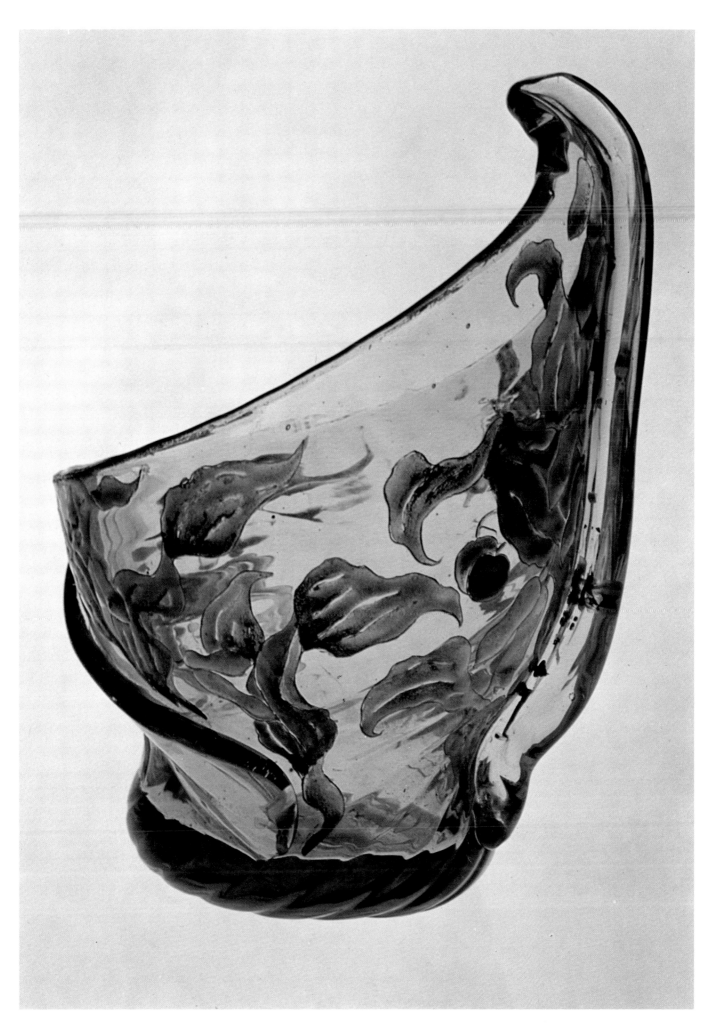

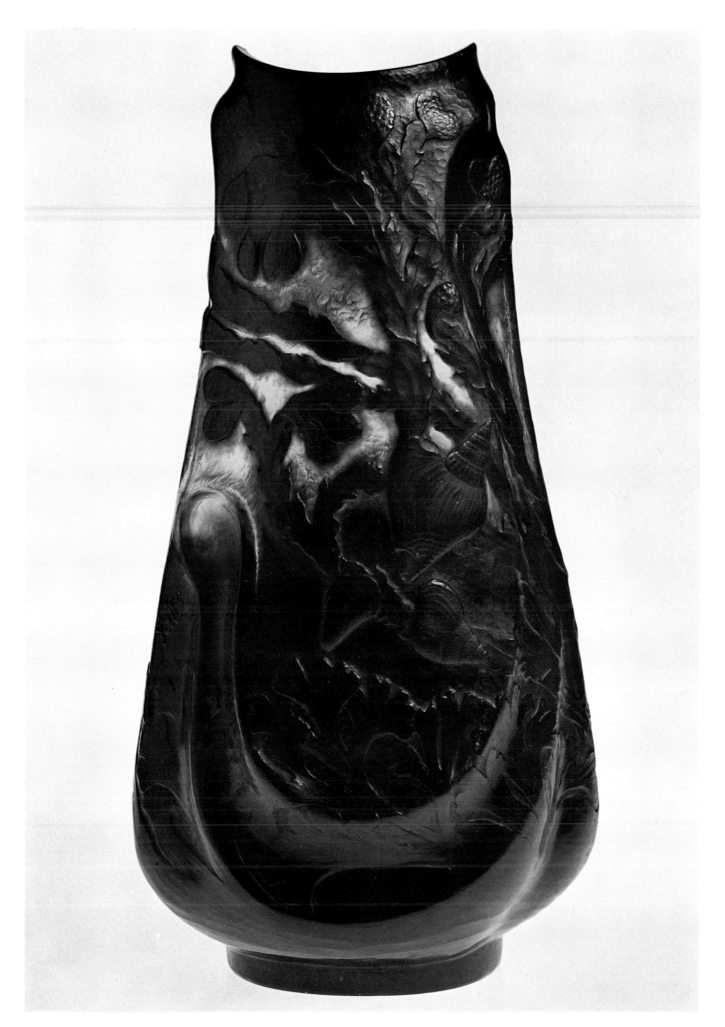

A Gallé marquetry vase with a bronze
base by Emile Gallé.
c. 1900.
13½ in. high.

Richard Dennis

Right
A Gallé marquetry vase.
c. 1900.
7¼ in. high.

Richard Dennis

In the 1870s and '80s a number of things could be said about European glass manufacture. Except in rare cases, and those mainly concerned with the reinterpretation of older traditions, supremacy in fine artistic glass ware had passed to Britain and America, where already forms and work-manship of glass showed a new awareness of the subtle potential of the material. European production of established commercial wares was enormous, but having concentrated for nearly a century on the decoration of glass as if it were porcelain, rather than on the intrinsic nature of the

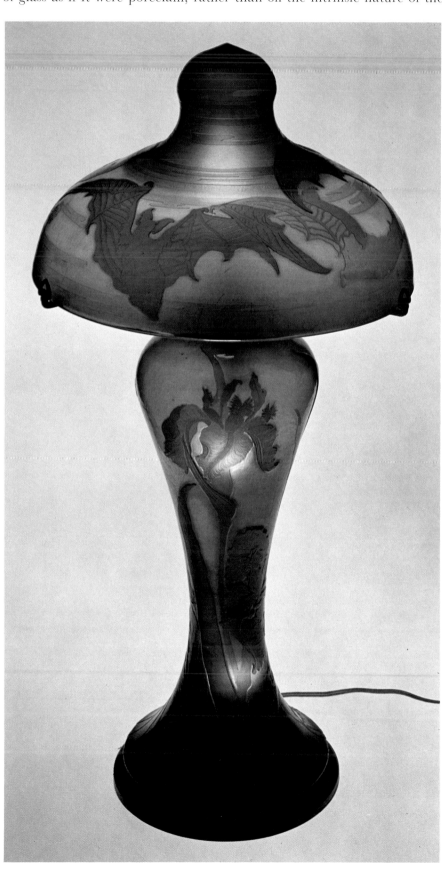

Left
A Gallé wine jug, showing carving and acid techniques.
c. 1900.
7½ in. high.

Richard Dennis

metal, Bohemian and French factories seemed to have forgotten the *raison d'être* of their art.

The intellectual movements which have been called variously *fin de siècle*, and 'the late Victorian revolt', had their artistic counterpart; and certainly, for the first time since the 16th century, the domestic art of glass making took place among the major arts—and was made almost the finest expression of the revolt of art nouveau. Partly because this glass making was the work of a few pioneer artists of great merit, and partly because

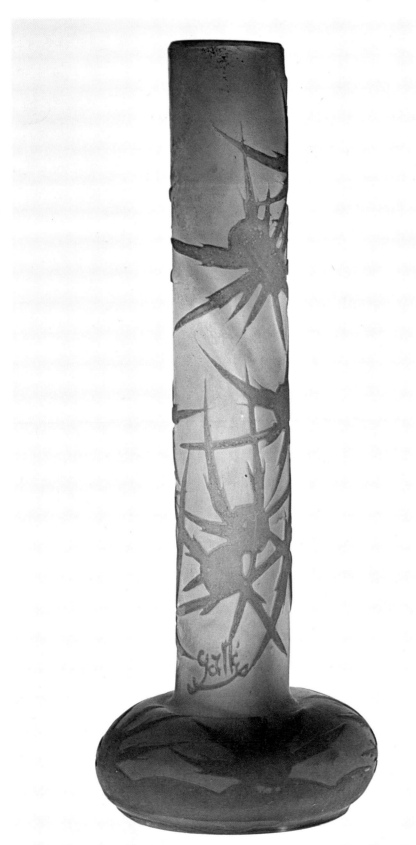

A post-Gallé vase of commercial production.
c. 1920.
8 in. high.

Richard Dennis

it was essentially a reaction against the commercial glass trade and the limitations of the market, it was nearly twenty years before it affected the general tenor of glass making in Europe. But after the famous Paris Exhibition in 1900, art nouveau penetrated the styles of nearly every factory and left them totally changed.

The origins of the new movement in glass are complex. The research lavished, largely at Government instigation, on glass technology in France and Bohemia, led not only to the more fanciful creations described in the last section, but also to the use of *pâte de verre*, new colours and iridescence. In France also, the best factories had turned by the 1850s to making freely moulded coloured glass ware with comparatively little surface decoration. The revivals of antiquity themselves served to acquaint the artists with the old techniques, and one of Gallé's earliest beakers is a straightforward pastiche of a 16th century German enamelled glass. The widespread disgust with industrialisation had already led to reinterpretations of the classical traditions, like those of Salviati; but probably the most significant stimulant was the 'discovery' of Japanese art in the 1860s.

A Daum overlay bowl.
c. 1908.
5 in. diameter.

J. Jesse

A Lalique seal in the form of an eagle's
head.
c. 1912.
3 in. high.

J. Jesse

A Lalique Easter egg.
c. 1912.
3 in. long.

J. Jesse

Left
A Daum mushroom lamp.
1925.
18 in. high.

J. Jesse

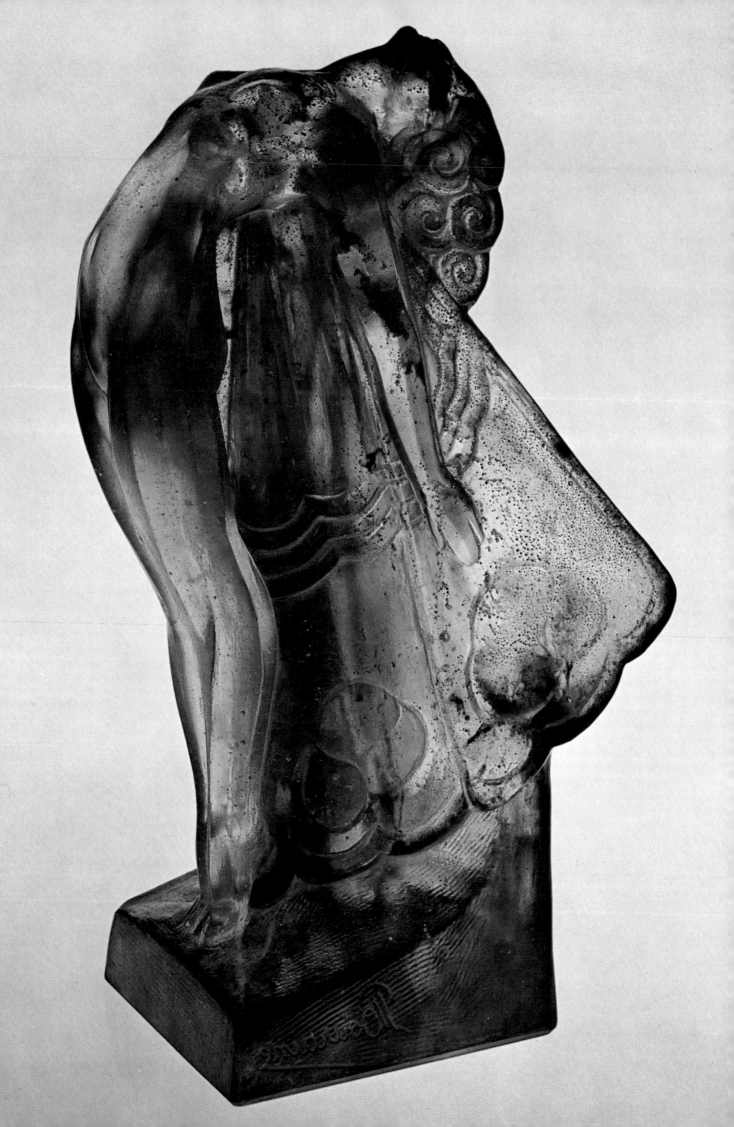

A bowl with serpent handles by Décorchemont.
1926.
12 in. diameter.

J. Jesse

Left
An Argy-Rousseau figure modelled by
Bouraine.
c. 1925
10 in. high.

J. Jesse

Old concepts of form and decoration were shattered by the asymmetrical, opaque vessels with their delicate colour and highly sophisticated linear and applied work.

In the artistic world of France, these diverse factors led to the forma- tion of 'L'Union Centrale des Arts Decoratif' which not only helped to found the Musée des Arts Decoratif, but organised exhibitions of con- temporary work. At one of these, in 1878, Emile Gallé and Eugène Rousseau first became known. Rousseau had originally worked on faience but he acquired a full knowledge of the technology of glass making and produced a fine, but limited, number of pieces between 1875 and 1885. Those which can be identified show strong Japanese influence, with oriental landscapes incised through coloured overlay, or flowers partly coloured and partly moulded into the body of the vessel, with great economy of line. His best known glasses resemble jade—a lightly coloured crackled substance, with streaks of flame red inside, moulded in large, almost monumental shapes.

Rousseau's work was little known at the time, but was carried on by his pupil, E. Lévillé, and others, who concentrated after 1900 on the crackled colour glaze in more fanciful, sometimes insipid, shapes. The artist who achieved most fame, indeed idolisation, in his own lifetime, was Emile Gallé (1846–1904) of Nancy, who had learnt the technology of glass in Germany. In 1878 he exhibited opaque, coloured and marbled glass and enamelled overlay with gold leaf between each casing. From then, until his most famous exhibition in 1889, he developed an original and lyrical style in almost every form of decorated glass. His chief innova- tions were the transformation of 'Japonisme' into a western idiom, the use of decorative lettering for inscriptions, and the evolution of a style

Three vases by Maurice Marinot.
1930s.

Corning Museum

Left
A vase by Maurice Marinot.
1910–1935.

Corning Museum

drawn from observed nature, in which the flowers, plants, insects and birds of his native countryside were transmuted into symbols of life itself. He borrowed ideas from mediaeval art and the 17th century skills of Bohemia and China; but he is notable in the history of glass above all for the way in which the works he exhibited at the beginning of the art nouveau movement captured the imagination because they seemed exactly to fulfil its aspirations. As a result, he became one of the foremost protagonists of art nouveau, and glass entered a new and higher phase of appreciation.

Opposite page
A bowl and glasses by Ehrenfeld.
Cologne, *c.* 1900.

Richard Dennis

114

The change was emphasised by his practice of signing his work; at once, each piece became unique, a collector's gem.

His work may be divided into three classes: the unique and rare pieces from his own hand, including the experimental and complex objects of the 1890s; the majority of overlay subjects with etched and engraved designs of flowers, leaves and trees, which he most probably designed; and the more conventional and repeated types made in his factory at Nancy. Something so individual was not easily fashioned for commercial production, although Gallé himself wrote in 1889 'neither I nor my workmen have found it impossible to reconcile cheap production with art . . .'.[11]

Gallé's work in the 1890s showed enormous enthusiasm and little decline in inventiveness. He was a polymath, a master of every decorative technique, and his display was the sensation of the 1900 Paris International Exhibition, which enshrined glass as a new art for the whole of Europe. After his death, his factory was continued by Victor Prouvé, and the motifs taken from nature and the lettering continued for several years. Gradually, commercial interpretation supervened. The essence of art nouveau

Four iridescent vases.
J. Lötz of Klostermühle, Austria, c. 1900.
J. Jesse

Right
A *Kelchglas* by Karl Kopping.
c. 1900.

Corning Museum

[11] Quoted in Ada Polak, *Modern Glass* (London, 1962), p. 28.

was, however, carried on by the Daum family, whose factory was also in Nancy, several of whose pieces are illustrated here. Elsewhere in France, Gallé's manner was followed with distinction, but after about 1905 inspiration seems to have declined.

In Germany, where the movement was called *Jugendstil*, a certain amount of glass ware was made to the designs of the painter, Karl Köpping, in Berlin. Immensely thin and elongated, they are based on the shapes of flowers and the emphasis here is much less on surface decoration than in France. Elsewhere, only L. C. Tiffany in New York reached the standard set by Rousseau and Gallé. In other forms of glass ware, French artists excelled: Joseph Brocard painted enamels in a remarkable modern version of Islamic glass, and a series of artists worked in *pâte de verre* after the revival of the skill by Henri Cros. Best known are the names of Albert Dammouse and Francis Décorchemont, both of whom began their careers as potters. Décorchemont moulded monumental bowls and vases in cloudy colours and his work suggests links with many facets of modern sculpture. Another aspect of art nouveau was the iridescent glass ware

Left
An enamelled scent bottle by Lobmeyr.
Vienna, *c*. 1891.

Richard Dennis

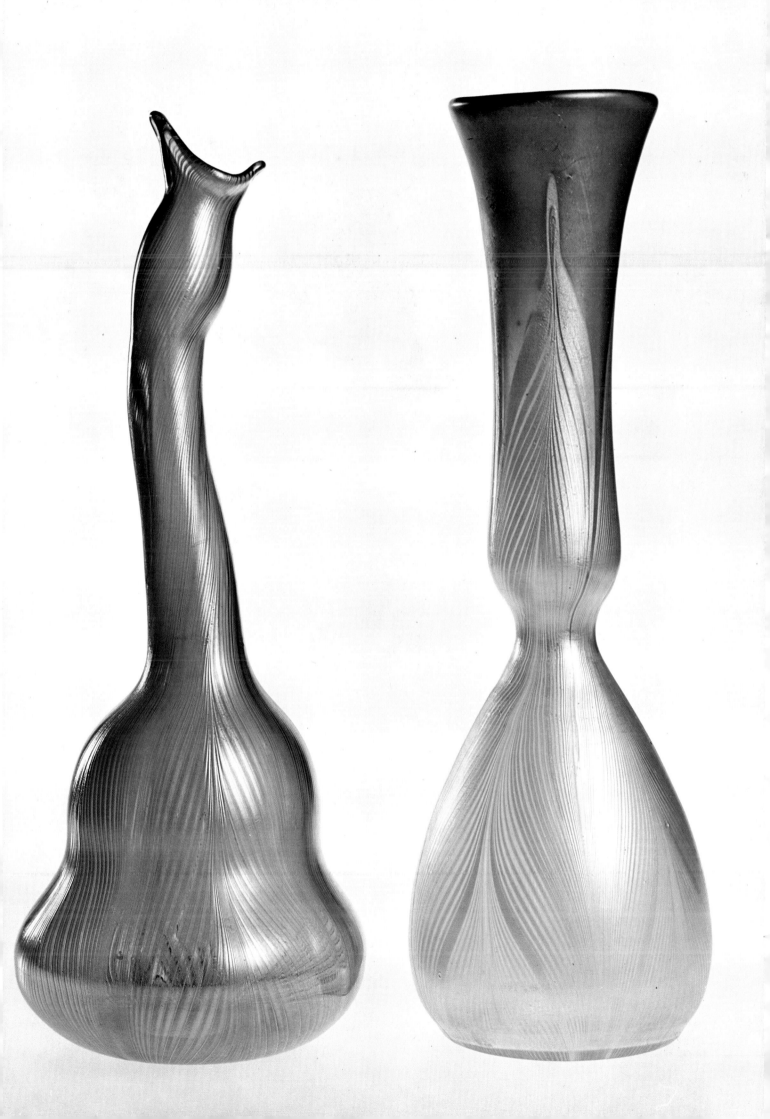

which the firm of J. Lötz'Witwe of Klostersmühle, in Bohemia, patented in 1898. A quantity of Bohemian iridescent ware was exhibited at Paris in 1900. Broncit-decor, a method of painting in matt black, usually in geometrical designs, was also evolved in Austria about 1910 and executed at the Viennese factory of Lobmeyr. Rather later, shading into the post-war period, the work of Réné Lalique developed from the art nouveau jewellery, which he exhibited in 1900, into a style of blown glass with splashed glazes, like Japanese pottery. After 1918, his factory produced the moulded frosted glass and opalescent ware which is one of the most famous idioms of the 1920s.

With the impact of the First World War, what could be called functional art, and the work of the Bauhaus school in Germany, the apparent unity of European style which had reached its 19th century peak in the art nouveau movement, disappeared. The next great Paris exhibition, in 1925, showed a variety of national styles. The primacy of France itself was challenged in the late 1920s and '30s by the artists of Orrefors in Sweden, and those of Denmark, Norway and Holland. At the same time, Venice underwent an artistic revival and the firms of Barovier and Venini turned in the 1930s to radical revision of classical tradition. In a text as short as this, an assessment of the modern era is scarcely possible. It is enough to say that colour remained an essential part of the finest glass made in Europe, despite the continued commercial fashion for table ware in clear and cut crystal.

Three iridescent vases by J. Lötz, two with silver overlay.
c. 1900.

J. Jesse